BFI Film Classics

The BFI Film Classics is a series of books that introduces, interprets and celebrates landmarks of world cinema. Each volume offers an argument for the film's 'classic' status, together with discussion of its production and reception history, its place within a genre or national cinema, an account of its technical and aesthetic importance, and in many cases, the author's personal response to the film.

For a full list of titles available in the series, please visit our website: <www.palgrave.com/bfi>

'Magnificently concentrated examples of flowing freeform critical poetry.'
Uncut

'A formidable body of work collectively generating some fascinating insights into the evolution of cinema.'
Times Higher Education Supplement

'The series is a landmark in film criticism.'
Quarterly Review of Film and Video

D0237870

Far From Heaven

John Gill

A BFI book published by Palgrave Macmillan

First published in 2011 by
PALGRAVE MACMILLAN

on behalf of the

BRITISH FILM INSTITUTE
21 Stephen Street, London W1T 1LN
www.bfi.org.uk

There's more to discover about film and television through the BFI. Our world-renowned archive, cinemas, festivals, films, publications and learning resources are here to inspire you.

Palgrave Macmillan in the UK is an imprint of Macmillan Publishers Limited, registered in England, company number 785998, of Houndmills, Basingstoke, Hampshire RG21 6XS. Palgrave Macmillan in the US is a division of St Martin's Press LLC, 175 Fifth Avenue, New York, NY 10010. Palgrave Macmillan is the global academic imprint of the above companies and has companies and representatives throughout the world. Palgrave® and Macmillan® are registered trademarks in the United States, the United Kingdom, Europe and other countries.

Series cover design: Ashley Western
Series text design: ketchup/SE14
Images from *Far From Heaven*, © Vulcan Productions/© Focus Features

Set by Cambrian Typesetters, Camberley, Surrey
Printed in China

This book is printed on paper suitable for recycling and made from fully managed and sustained forest sources. Logging, pulping and manufacturing processes are expected to conform to the environmental regulations of the country of origin.

British Library Cataloguing-in-Publication Data
A catalogue record for this book is available from the British Library
A catalog record for this book is available from the Library of Congress
10 9 8 7 6 5 4 3 2 1
20 19 18 17 16 15 14 13 12 11

ISBN 978–1–84457–287–8

Contents

One

Counterfeit and reproduction imply always an anguish, a disquieting
foreignness: the uneasiness before the photograph, considered like a witch's
trick – and more generally before any technical apparatus, which is always an
apparatus of reproduction, related by [Walter] Benjamin to the uneasiness
before the mirror-image. There is already sorcery at work in the mirror.

Jean Baudrillard, 'The Orders of Simulacra', in *Simulations*
(New York: Semiotext(e), 1983), p. 153

These observations on the nature of representation from the late
grand jester of postmodernism might be recommended as handy
carry-on luggage for anyone setting off to explore the films of Todd
Haynes. They resonate even in *Far From Heaven*, seemingly his most
straightforward film to date, yet one which, as we shall see, is also
bound up in the notions of the counterfeit, implicit anguish and
disquieting foreignness, unease before the photograph, and the
sorcery already at work in the mirror – here that of the cinema
screen.

The premise of *Far From Heaven* at first appears quite simple:
a perfect suburban Connecticut housewife, Cathy Whitaker (Julianne
Moore), discovers that her perfect suburban Connecticut husband,
Frank (Dennis Quaid), has two profound problems: he's a closet
queer, and is hitting the bottle with his morning coffee at the office to
dull the pain. The very first time we meet Frank, he is sitting in the
local police station wadding a handkerchief in his hands while the
cops call Cathy to come and bail him out. Frank has been busted,
mistakenly, he claims, for 'loitering'. Cathy is as adamant as Frank
that he is innocent, but as we will see, this is not his first adventure
into the shadowy underworld of the mid-century North American
homosexual, nor will it be his last. Similar to the narrative of a John
Cheever story, this event will have ramifications for everyone around

him, and ultimately leave Cathy, and us, wondering if she is doing the wifely thing of standing by her man, or is perhaps the victim of a far more profound social malaise.

As their perfect 1957 Hartford Christmas celebrations start to unravel around her, Cathy finds solace in the friendship offered by their African-American gardener, Raymond Deagan (Dennis Haysbert). Both relationships – marriage and friendship – are heading for a collision with the mores of the era, in a tiny, almost Joycean (vide *Dubliners*, and in particular his 'The Dead') story of domestic 'paralysis', where the hypocrisy and small-town spite of period and place are laid bare. All three leading characters – Cathy, Frank, Raymond – are about to commit acts of betrayal or abandonment, or be abandoned or betrayed themselves, but only we the audience understand the full import of their actions.

One of the many strengths of *Far From Heaven* is that it works and can be appreciated on any number of levels. (Incidentally, it was the director's choice to use all upper case in the title, which, along with the hysterical italic typography typical of the film posters of the era, in a logo and typeface designed by Haynes himself, is perhaps one of the many sly conceits packed into this film.) Ostensibly, it is a bizarre love triangle, and one from which all three parties will emerge

Dulling the pain with the first coffee of the day

Never simply a staircase: Cathy and periwinkle-blue light descend the religious space of the stairwell

damaged. Set in the late 1950s, it sports the appurtenances of the classic 'women's film': marriage, fidelity, infidelity, love across race and class barriers, and love within gender constraints. It is cast in the mould of the classic films of Douglas Sirk and his era, and even alludes to specific Sirk films, notably in its borrowings from *All That Heaven Allows* (1955). The crucial difference, however, is that the taboo subjects that Sirk was forced to keep implicit, because of the morality of the times or simply the rulings of the Production Code (which explicitly forbade any references to adultery, homosexuality, miscegenation, and more), are made blazingly explicit in *Far From Heaven*. However, even here, as Haynes himself explained, there are two distinctions in the film, between the treatment of race and the treatment of homosexuality. This distinction between the implicit and explicit spurred its most perceptive British reviewer, Peter Bradshaw of the *Guardian*, to declare, perhaps a little rashly, that Haynes had in fact invented an entirely new genre of film.[1] It is the purpose of this book to explore Bradshaw's claim, and those of others who saw a great deal more going on in *Far From Heaven* than initially meets the eye.

Far From Heaven could have been a very different film if Haynes had pursued an earlier idea for his next project after *Velvet Goldmine* (1998). In a public discussion with David Schwartz, chief curator at New York's Museum of the Moving Image, Haynes revealed that his first idea for the film was a melodrama about a married actor who falls in with a group of gay Hollywood actors who help him up the career ladder but in doing so create tensions between him and his wife. Only the wife's primary point of view and the subtext of bisexuality or unacknowledged homosexuality would remain as the project developed.

After the critical and, with the latter at least, financial disappointments of *[safe]* (1995) and *Velvet Goldmine*, Haynes took the best part of a year off, during which time he painted, read the whole of Proust and pondered his next step. *The New York Times* wrote that Haynes went into 'a deep funk' in this period, reporting a friend as saying 'Velvet Goldmine almost killed him.'[2] As Haynes has revealed in a number of interviews, after fifteen years in New York he had grown tired of living in the city, and at the beginning of 2000 got in his car and drove across the country to Portland, where his sister had found him a house. Rejuvenated by the city's alternative culture (it is home to, variously, a thriving rep/indie cinema scene, a lively LGBT community and more post-punk bands than you can shake a stick at), Haynes settled in to write. He finished the first draft of Far From Heaven in just ten days. 'The script poured out of me,' he told the LA Weekly. 'Which of course made me completely mistrust it. I thought, "This must be crap." '[3]

Undeterred, he and longtime producer Christine Vachon began work on a production plan for Far From Heaven with a budget pitched at $14 million, more than double that of Velvet Goldmine. Even with admirers such as George Clooney and Steven Soderbergh aboard as executive producers (a largely nominal credit, there to sprinkle some stardust on a film proposal), it only managed to pull together $12 million from assorted backers (chiefly Miramax), a figure that would exercise Vachon's budget-juggling skills and earn her assembled crew the warning, 'We have more ambition than money.'[4]

Faced with a $2 million-dollar budget 'haircut' (Vachon's simile for the funding problems with Velvet Goldmine), filming of Far From Heaven was fraught. Shooting began in New Jersey just after the 2001 World Trade Center attack, which took two weeks out of a planned six-week pre-production schedule. As is commonplace, scenes were shot out of sequence, as and when cast and crew could be assembled (Dennis Haysbert commuted between New York and Los Angeles, where he was simultaneously filming the television series 24). In the last two weeks of its two-month shoot, the film's bond company, which insures a film against unseen financial problems, took over production, concerned that Haynes would run over budget (director and crew worked eighteen-hour days instead). At one point, Haynes and Vachon had to play a game of hide-and-seek with their backers, filming crucial later scenes first to ensure that others would have to be shot for the sake of narrative cohesion. Cast and crew sometimes worked until five in the morning in freezing conditions that took them some way beyond any contractual and union obligations, which makes *Far From Heaven*'s look of unhurried elegance all the more remarkable.

Critics, admirers and not a few enemies – the blogosphere seethed with vitriol directed at both film and director at the time – have pursued Haynes for a 'definitive' reading of *Far From Heaven* since its release, but it may well be that the film ultimately eludes any single definitive interpretation beyond its 'surface' reading as a period romantic melodrama. It is this reading that kept audiences around the world (it was promptly dubbed into Spanish, as *Lejos del cielo*, for the sizeable global Hispanic market[5]) alert for its 103 minutes of doomed love, small-town intrigue, strange weather, fabulous frocks and a sumptuous full orchestral score from Elmer Bernstein. It is probably the same reading that inspired its nomination for four Oscars, four Golden Globes and led to Julianne Moore winning the Best Actress award at the Venice Film Festival in 2003.

Yet, as Peter Bradshaw and others were already intuiting, this was not simply another period romantic melodrama. Haynes himself had planted enough seemingly 'intertextual' references in the film, in scenes, situations and techniques that alluded to earlier films and genres, to suggest that there was more going on below the surface reading, and film buffs and cineastes were quick to pick up on the allusions to Sirk and other film-makers besides.

Then the cinephiles and academics set to work, dismantling the film shot by shot, frame by frame, angle by angle, and sometimes even word by word, to mine a deeper film than the one we thought we'd seen at the cinema. This 'new' film did not contradict the 'first' film, but rather augmented it with new, if unconfirmed, layers of possible meaning, and certainly a multitude of interpretations. Haynes has at times played a rather fey game of denial when interrogated about the film, quite adamantly refuting, for example,

that it was either ironic, or pastiche, less still a paean to a particular genre. At one point, Haynes and Julianne Moore explained this in a public Q&A filmed for a 'making-of' short to accompany the DVD release, the latter insisting, 'There is *no* irony' in *Far From Heaven*, although Haynes allowed there might be 'some' subtext at work in the film. Numerous critics and academics have weighed in with their theories elevating it to the level of allegory, postmodern parlour game, even a deconstructionist marvel.

After all this rough critical manhandling, *Far From Heaven* has become a floating text – that is, one that has set itself adrift from conventional reading, association, comparison, even the conventions of film-making themselves, a *sui generis* work that has to be taken on its own terms. It is entirely possible that, the closer we look, *Far From Heaven* may in fact turn out to be what Roland Barthes would have called an 'empty sign', that is – and Haynes the semiology graduate quite clearly brought his library of Critical Theory to the making of *Far From Heaven* – what might be crudely described as a semiotic cocktease, a sign appearing to contain signification, but in fact empty of the signified. This is not, in itself, necessarily a bad thing, and may indeed add to our enjoyment of the film. Certainly, Haynes has left enough evidence lying around in the movie for the sign hunter to have a lot of fun and not a little mischief with *Far From Heaven*; perhaps as much, in fact, as Haynes had when planting the evidence there in the first place.

The key question, of course, is whether or not you need to pick up on the allusions and references to fully appreciate *Far From Heaven*. As Mary Ann Doane pertinently asks in her essay 'Pathos and Pathology: The Cinema of Todd Haynes' (in the *Camera Obscura* collection of scholarly essays, *A Magnificent Obsession*), 'is it necessary to know the source in order to grasp the work of citation? Is the perfect spectator for these films the alert cinephile with a specialized and somewhat arcane knowledge?'[6] The answer, of course, is no. But if Haynes has booby-trapped his film with references, allusion and devices borrowed from Brecht's idea of 'Verfremdungseffekt' (the 'alienation effect' that makes the viewer step back and reconsider exactly what they are watching) and probably also Barthes's observation that 'realist' art in fact relies on artifice, then we owe it to ourselves, to Haynes and to the film itself to go looking for them.

Two

Their homes are their prisons. They are imprisoned even by the tastes of the society in which they live. In *All That Heaven Allows* this woman is imprisoned by her home, her family, her society. They are imprisoned in two ways – by their personal habits, and by the class to which they belong.

> Douglas Sirk, interviewed in Jane and Michael Stern, 'Two Weeks in Another Town', *Bright Lights Film Journal*, no. 6 (1977)

If there is intertextuality – one work interacting with the ideas of another – at play in *Far From Heaven*, then Sirk's description of the malaise that is central to his films, and by extension to Haynes's, surely touches on the essence of the intertextual transaction between the two directors, specifically their treatment of life in suburbia.

Suburbia has always produced its share of discontents, although perhaps it took the appearance of a spate of 'anti-suburbia' films in recent decades – from the white picket fences of David Lynch's *Blue Velvet* (1986) to the spookily quiet avenues of Sam Mendes's *Revolutionary Road* (2008), via Haynes's own *[safe]*, Mendes's *American Beauty* (1999) and Paul Thomas Anderson's *Magnolia* (1999), among others – to inspire no less an authority than the *Wall Street Journal* to run an article complaining, 'Why Does Hollywood Hate the Suburbs?'[7] Hollywood was, of course, only following the printed word's disdain for what Allen Ginsberg called the 'invisible suburbs', a disdain that can be tracked back through not just Cheever and Updike, but anyone with a mind to satirise the middle classes, a desire as old as class itself.

Yet neither Haynes nor Sirk actually seems to show disdain for suburbia itself, which many of Sirk's North American viewers would have regarded as their rightful entitlement after a world war and a period of postwar austerity. Their target, rather, is the society of which suburbia is just a symptom. The territory that Haynes evokes so convincingly, in fact so lovingly, in *Far From Heaven*, is a modern-day Cockaigne fitted out with all the latest time-saving gadgets, although, as we will see, there is already sorcery afoot in the image. Todd Haynes is about to unleash several monsters in this seeming paradise.

Far From Heaven is set in the identifiably extant town of Hartford, Connecticut (the birthplace of none other than Katharine Hepburn), even though most of the filming was executed, probably due to budgetary constraints, in various sites around New Jersey. While it is set in a cinematic Hartford, what we see on screen is not Hartford; what little we see of the exterior in this essentially housebound movie is a necessarily fictionalised locale bearing little similarity to Hartford either in the 1950s or today, when gleaming skyscrapers dominate this small city's Hudson River frontage.

It is approaching Christmas – or not, if you keep an eye on the weather through the movie, although a very Joycean snow begins to fall as Haynes's melodrama approaches its gloomy conclusion – and

Hartford society scions Cathy and Frank Whitaker are readying
themselves and their household (two children, David [Ryan Ward]
and Janice [Lindsay Andretta], and their African-American maid,
Sibyl [Viola Davis]) for Christmas. So far, so Frank Capra, until one
evening, Frank, a senior marketing executive at the Magnatech
television manufacturing corporation, does not return from work in
time to leave for an important dinner date at the home of friends.
The telephone – an instrument that will take on a life of its own in
the film – rings, and a worried Sybil passes it to Cathy explaining that
it's the police on the line. Frank is being held, for reasons unstated,
and needs Cathy to vouch for him. Cathy rushes to the police station,
to be told that Frank has been detained for what appears to be
'loitering' (listen carefully as she enters the police station and you'll
hear a cop in the background saying, almost as though hoping Cathy
will hear, 'Big-time faggot. Family man. Never can tell.').
Cathy instinctively sides with Frank, who insists, with a mixture of
anguish and anger, that it was all a case of mistaken identity.
Cathy drives him home, solicitous in the face of his indignation,
and tucks him up in bed. Frank sighs, 'I'm so tired,' but for reasons
we may already suspect, and which will become explicit later,
this may be a tactic for avoiding sexual contact with his wife.

The telephone, a device that will take on a life of its own, delivers the message that
will cause a train-wreck

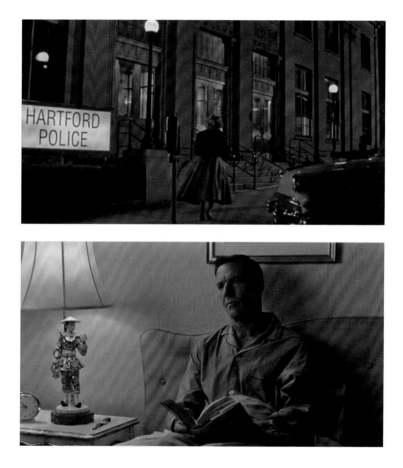

It is 'portfolio season' at Magnatech, when the corporation's marketing executives roll out their new campaign designs, and the pressure of work keeps Frank at the office so late and so often that even the children are starting to complain. As if this weren't bad enough, Cathy is busy organising the annual Magnatech party, traditionally held at the delightful Whitaker home, with the help of her best friend, Eleanor (Patricia Clarkson), and they haven't even decided on the colour scheme for the party yet.

Cathy heads to retrieve her 'big-time faggot' from the cops; Frank isn't in the mood

Although nothing is said about it, the garden has also been getting a little out of control, a fact made apparent by the appearance of a new gardener, Raymond Deagan, in the back garden just when Cathy is being interviewed by the society editor of the local *Hartford Weekly Gazette*. (The interview is clearly a device intended to establish Cathy's pre-eminence – her lovely home, her lovely children, her lovely husband, her lovely life – in this spookily sterile American suburb.) While Cathy is shocked – '*What on Earth?*' she gasps – at the sight of a large African-American man outside her French windows, and the society editor clearly believes a crime is about to take place ('Perhaps you should call the police ...'), all is explained when the stranger introduces himself as the son of her regular gardener, who has died. In fact, Raymond's appearance is flagged by the large gardener's carry-all, the words 'Deagan Gardens' clearly visible on its side as he places the bag on the garden table, but Cathy mysteriously overlooks this fairly obvious intervention from the props department. Already, Haynes is flagging the fact that something is askew; whatever the circumstances, Cathy should surely have been aware that her gardener was either unwell or heard that he had just died.

As portfolio season drags on, keeping Frank at the office all hours, Cathy decides one evening to take him some food.

Guinevere and Lancelot in her garden

The press camera appears in Cathy's home uninvited; the housewife at bay; like a lamb to the slaughter

Entering the darkened building and explaining her mission to the
security guard, she makes her way to Frank's office, wrapped meal
in hand, and sure enough there's a chink of light under his door.
Expecting Frank to be slaving over a new marketing presentation,
she opens the office door to find him in a passionate kiss with
another man. Stunned, she flees, dropping the meal as she runs to
the elevator.

That kiss – it barely lasts three seconds, but is possibly one of
the most homoerotic moments in the history of cinema, and one in
which both parties keep all their clothes on – is not only the moment
of Cathy's undoing, but of Frank's, too. It will also impact on at
least five other lives as well: Raymond, his daughter Sarah (Jordan
Puryear), the Whitaker children, Sybil and the lover Frank will later
meet, Kenny (Nicholas Joy), although Kenny is only ever identified
in the on-screen credits as 'Blond Boy' [sic] and is never given a
name in the script beyond some familial chit-chat by a swimming
pool in Miami. It will impact, indirectly, on 'best friend' Eleanor,
and most of the Whitakers' social circle besides, if only vicariously,
as the subject of gossip, a scandal that will send ripples through both
the middle-class white community and the working-class African-
American community. Each of these groups will have a ready

Frank's working late again ...

… or maybe not. Edward Lachman's camera tips sideways as Cathy flees through the periwinkle-blue gloom

opinion of the friendship that develops between Cathy and Raymond, some of those opinions expressed with rocks hurled through Raymond's windows at night by his African-American neighbours. The white community will content themselves with feasting on the gossip about Cathy's unseemly friendship with a African-American man from a lower-class background, and, presumably, later, off screen, about Frank's decision to pursue the true, homosexual, nature of his desires.

The melodrama and backdrop will be familiar territory to anyone versed in the films of Sirk and his contemporaries, or who has read either the novels or short stories of John Cheever (*The Wapshot Scandal* [1964] involves a similar same-sex scandal set in a similar time and place) or the steamier Grace Metalious novel, *Peyton Place* (1956), later made into both a film (1957) and a popular television series. What marks *Far From Heaven* as different from the outset is that it is a film, in the words of scholar Marcia Landy, 'cast in the historical context of the 1950s but contaminated by the present' (in her essay 'Storytelling and Information in Todd Haynes' Films', in *The Cinema of Todd Haynes: All That Heaven Allows*).[8] What Peter Bradshaw saw as a 'new genre' is, then, a period melodrama perfect in its observation of the conventions of the genre but which addresses its core issues – homosexuality and miscegenation, the institutional misogyny of the era, and the homophobia, racism and sexism they engender in others – in a thoroughly explicit, contemporary, manner. This is the first hint that Haynes may have had an altogether subtler agenda to hand when writing and filming *Far From Heaven*. Some observers will even go as far as describing the narrative and *mise en scène* as little more than window dressing for Haynes's deeper intent, the dismantling of the mechanism of storytelling itself, and the disruption of the assumed intimacies between storyteller and audience.

Three

The text of Cervantes and that of Menard are verbally identical, but the second is almost infinitely richer.

Jorge Luis Borges, 'Pierre Menard, Author of the *Quixote*', in *Ficciones*
(London: Weidenfeld & Nicolson, 1962), p. 42

For some viewers, Haynes's references to the films of Sirk and others are almost comically obvious, notably the deliberate echoes of the tensions played out in *All That Heaven Allows*. Cathy's friendship with her gardener is a direct quote from the earlier film, in which Jane Wyman's Cary Scott falls in love with (white) gardener Ron Kirby (Rock Hudson), right down to the woodland scene when Raymond-qua-Ron proffers Cathy-qua-Cary a sprig of flowering witch hazel by the pond (although in the script it is variously a Quaking Aspen and later a Silver-tip spruce).

Haynes also references other films beyond those of Sirk, notably Max Ophüls's *The Reckless Moment* (1949) (not least the scene where a distraught Cathy throws herself on her bed, which Haynes says is a deliberate reference to Ophüls's film) and his earlier *Letter from an Unknown Woman* (1948), specifically the farewell scene at the railway station. Further investigation of *The Reckless Moment* might suggest, as we will see when we consider Haynes's treatment of the family and his rarefied lighting techniques, that Ophüls's film could be considered as a companion piece to *Far from Heaven* – more so even, perhaps, than *All That Heaven Allows*. In simple narrative terms, both movies are about a woman facing a dilemma unaided and finding emotional support from an unlikely exterior source. Both feature an African-American maid called Sibyl who says 'Do you want me to go with you?' at a moment of crisis, and both have a son called David who is nagged (to almost comedic effect in the Ophüls) by his mother. These, however, are droll little *hommages* from one director to another. The theme of a woman alone coping with family life without the aid of a user's manual runs deeper, and recurs in most of the other touchstone films that Haynes cites as his key influences.

Two ideas of interest to those suspicious of Haynes's narrative intent spring to mind here. The first is Borges's mischievous digression on the fictional Pierre Menard, who rewrites Cervantes's *Don Quixote*, word-for-word verbatim, but *totally differently*. The second is Umberto Eco's notion of the simulacrum, possibly borrowed from Jean Baudrillard. The simulacrum, explored in Eco's *Faith in Fakes* (1986, aka *Travels in Hyperreality*), is the better-than-the-original copy, the forged version of *The Last Supper* or the Venus de Milo, often executed in bizarrely inappropriate materials, rendered harmless, or less disturbing, by the act of replication (some later versions of the Venus de Milo, for example, have mysteriously acquired arms). *Far From Heaven* can hardly be described as harmless or less disturbing, but in using the techniques of the genre he is quoting from to construct a lexicon of gestures and effects (not least the rear-window projections visible in Cathy's various car journeys, a technology not seen in Hollywood for decades), Haynes has effectively rewritten Sirk – verbatim but totally differently. He has fashioned a simulacrum of the period melodrama, but with completely different materials, not least the modern film technology unavailable to those earlier film-makers (even though Haynes has, to use a neologism, 'antiqued' some of that technology or, in the case of one of Cathy's car journeys, actually used an original rear projection taken from a print of *All That Heaven Allows*). *Far From Heaven* thus becomes an 'old-fashioned' movie but one filtered through a thoroughly modern, even postmodern, sensibility.

Since they are in effect Todd Haynes's building materials, it is also worth noting that Sirk's films themselves have, in the ongoing critical reappraisal or renovation of his work, taken on a postmodern sheen. Regarded in their day as little more than tawdry tearjerkers, and quite cheerfully dismissed as 'merely' women's movies, they and, in particular, their director, were adopted by the

Cahiers du cinéma coterie in the late 1950s (Jean-Luc Godard declared himself an admirer in 1959). By 1967, when *Cahiers* dedicated an entire edition to Sirk, his status as auteur was confirmed (and some eight years after Sirk had retired from Hollywood, largely, it would seem, out of disgust with the system). The following year, the great North American proponent of auteur theory, Andrew Sarris, published his seminal *The American Cinema*, in which he famously said of Sirk, 'Time, if nothing else, will vindicate Douglas Sirk'[9] (interesting alone for its implication that, in 1968, Douglas Sirk needed to be 'vindicated' of anything). Britain's *Screen* magazine followed suit in 1971,[10] presaging a Sirk retrospective at the following year's Edinburgh Film Festival. His apotheosis was complete in 1977 when New York's Museum of Modern Art staged its own major retrospective, conferring gallery-object status on the hitherto lowly 'women's film'. Opinions on the Sirk canon vary, depending on individual reactions to his approach to melodrama, but the most balanced is probably that of, again, Andrew Sarris: 'I would not rationalize his career as trash transcended or corn camped up. There is irony in the tension between his style and his basic material, but it is an irony that is neither condescending nor dialectical.'[11]

The Magnatech party, when things really start to go downhill

Others have pointed out that Haynes's 1950s – and *Far From Heaven* is set quite specifically in the winter of 1957–8 – are not quite what they seem, either. Many of the film's critics, Sarris among them, point out that the 1950s (Sarris's 'favourite movie-making decade') were far from anodyne, gifting us films such as *Sunset Boulevard* (1950) and *Sweet Smell of Success* (1957). Todd McGowan, in his essay 'Relocating Our Enjoyment of the 1950s: The Politics of Fantasy in *Far From Heaven*' (also from *The Cinema of Todd Haynes*), argues that 'most Hollywood films turn to the decade in order to emphasize its stultifying and oppressive character', and goes on to say that 'it becomes tempting to classify [*Far From Heaven*] as a realistic critique of the nostalgic conservative fantasy of the 1950s'.[12] Tempting, maybe, but, as McGowan believes, wrong. Haynes himself explained his intentions to *Salon* magazine thus: 'We wanted to suggest that the 1950s bear a far more disturbing resemblance to today's society than we generally want to admit.'[13] And, as he told Geoffrey O'Brien in *ArtForum* magazine, the film is built 'out of the language of 50s cinema, not from the 50s' themselves.[14]

This would suggest that *Far From Heaven* does in fact have a didactic agenda, even if Haynes conceals it behind the blizzard of pink and red silks and taffetas of Sandy Powell's all-stops-out costumery. The director is very careful in date-tying his narrative to the autumn of 1957, with the town's Ritz cinema showing *Three Faces of Eve* (1957) and *Miracle in the Rain* (1956); while later, Frank watches President Dwight D. Eisenhower on television discussing the Little Rock Central High School desegregation stand-off. This pinpoints the start of Haynes's melodrama to September 1957, when US Army troops were sent to Little Rock to escort African-American pupils past local National Guardsmen who were blocking them from entering the high school on the orders of controversial governor Orval Faubus. This also clearly sites the film in the build-up to events such as the Selma to Montgomery marches of 1965, when the micro-events portrayed

in Hartford, such as a Magnatech party guest declaring 'There are no blacks' in Hartford (despite the evidence to the contrary standing around in cocktail-party livery and holding trays of canapés), would become the macro-events of Selma and Montgomery, flashing across the nation's television screens and newspaper front pages.

Haynes works the race issue into every nook and cranny of his narrative: from the appearance of two nice folks from the National Association for the Advancement of Colored People (NAACP) on Cathy's front doorstep, to her telling Raymond, 'My husband and I have always believed in equal rights for the Negro' and to Frank's racist outburst when news of Cathy's friendship with Raymond scandalises his fellow Magnatech executives, and elsewhere besides. Hence Haynes's comments about the perhaps unrealised similarities between the 1950s and the 2000s, when the African-American Harvard academic Henry Louis Gates Jr could still be arrested for attempting to get into his own home because a white woman thought he was breaking into the sort of house where African-American people don't normally live.[15]

Interestingly, however, the other key dynamic at work in *Far From Heaven*, same-sex love, is treated very differently, perhaps in

Nope, definitely no blacks in Hartford

acknowledgment of the mores of the era – homosexuals could 'pass', whereas African-American people clearly could not – but also because Haynes wants to take Frank's story in other directions, directions that will only be revealed as the narrative progresses (even though he places most of this narrative strand off screen). Haynes told one interviewer:

It became clear as I was writing the script that the theses of sexuality and race were counterbalances, with the woman as the force separating them. One was condemned to secrecy and the other to a public backdrop; one was buried within the domestic setting and the other was visible and open to rampant projection.[16]

Thus, as the two main narrative strands proceed in tandem, and will become causally intertwined (Cathy, betrayed by Frank, tells Eleanor that her friendship with Raymond 'made me feel ... alive somewhere', and later suggests to Raymond that in fact maybe they should run away together), they follow entirely different arcs through the film. While Haynes wears his race card on his sleeve – Raymond becomes in effect a Buddha-like figure, given to gnomic utterances, poetic quotation, philosophical gravitas and an unusually fine appreciation of Abstract Expressionist art for someone from his background – he plays a far more ambiguous, perhaps even dangerous, game in his treatment of Frank, his sexuality and the world in which he explores it. Frank is revealed, ultimately, as an utterly selfish coward, prepared to destroy a family in pursuit of his own happiness. Haynes, perhaps with the ghost of Jonathan Swift looking over his shoulder as he wrote, portrays the seedy world of the invert – the shadowy stairways leading to cinema men's rooms (it would be impertinent, and against the genre, for the camera to press any further), the low-lit no-name back-alley bars where perverts gathered to drown their sorrows – in much the way that the muckraking media of the era would have portrayed it. (Although Frank's cinema visit in fact

Haynes submerges Frank in his hyper-real palette. Is the Family Man a stranger to this milieu or already a seasoned traveller in the queer underworld?

points at another intertextual source, Edward Hopper's painting *New York Movie* of 1939, the first of two visual echoes of the artist's work in *Far From Heaven*.)

Neither Frank and his cohorts nor the places where they forgather are compelling exemplars of the 'gay pride' that was beginning to develop, albeit in inchoate form, in groups such as the Mattachine Society and the lesbian Daughters of Bilitis, which were contemporaneous to the NAACP; the Mattachine Society was formed in Los Angeles in 1950 and was active on both coasts by the middle of the decade. (There is also plenty of first-hand evidence from the era, not least in the lauded documentary *Before Stonewall* [1984], directed by Greta Schiller and Robert Rosenberg.) Yet the Los Angeles Black Cat Bar riots of 1967, which predated the famous Stonewall riots of 1969, occurred less than a decade after the events portrayed in *Far From Heaven*. Even then, North American homosexuals were slowly building the happy lives that Cathy briefly hopes she and Raymond might establish for themselves – but that, of course, for either Frank and His Friends or for Cathy and Raymond, would be heresy against the conventions of Haynes's chosen genre.

Cathy, Frank and Dr Bowman, with Frank's face a study of mute terror at what may lie in store

Four

'I tried so hard to make it go away.'

Frank

Frank's problem, as his psychiatrist Dr Bowman (James Rebhorn) would no doubt have told him, is that he wasn't trying hard enough. Yet in Frank's last scene in the film, when he calls Cathy and calmly discusses meeting to talk over their divorce plans – a conversation of breathtaking banality, and perhaps intentionally so – he's already installed in a hotel room with 'Blond Boy' from the Miami scenes.

Frank's belated acceptance of his sexuality and his breezy disregard for US law in checking into a hotel with Blond Boy (in 1958, most hotel clerks would have been calling the cops before they had time to put their bags down) are just some of the many anomalies in *Far From Heaven*. Haynes's script has already informed us of Frank's seemingly impeccable credentials as a Family Man. Asked if he's OK driving home after a drink with some work colleagues (a scene accompanied by one of Bernstein's themes transposed as a sleazy blues with walking bass), Frank mannishly

Our one glimpse of Frank's off-screen confessions to Dr Bowman

quips, 'Thank you, Davis, but as the second-in-command of the USS *McMillan*, I do feel able to locate my own car,' which tells us he's seen action as a senior officer in the Navy, perhaps during the recent Korean War. He's Hartford's number one golfer as well, adored by everyone who works with or under him, and while he may not have made it to Madison Avenue yet, he is clearly regarded as the golden boy of Magnatech. He and Cathy are hailed as Mr and Mrs Magnatech – a framed company ad, featuring a couple resembling the Whitakers, hangs on the wall of their lounge, where in earlier times a crucifix or family portrait might have hung – although we rarely see them actually watching the television. Perhaps mere ownership of the device is sufficient proof of dedication to the Magnatech empire.

Over the Christmas of 1957, matters in their Hartford dream home start to fall apart, and very fast. Frank's secret life as, in the words of the cop, a 'big-time faggot' is revealed suddenly and without any backstory early in the film's first act. Later, when he and Cathy are awkwardly discussing his predicament, he admits, 'Once, a long time ago, I had problems,' although we are left none the wiser as to what these problems were, or why they might have resurfaced now. Given the circumstances of Frank's fall from grace, we might

Although we may suspect Frank's reasons for agreeing to undergo 'therapy'

assume that the 'problems' in fact never went away at all, and that the only real problem now is that he has been found out. If the film's timeframe is linear and without lacunae of days or weeks, Frank is out cruising for sex the night after his arrest, which would suggest that he is a fairly persistent cruiser when the opportunity arises. In his negotiations of the landscape of homosexuality – the men's rooms in cinemas showing films that no Family Man would go to see alone (*Three Faces of Eve*? How 'gay' can you get out on your own in 1950s Connecticut?), the bars where the subterraneans lurk – he also seems to know where to find the action in a small town like Hartford, where everybody's secrets would be everybody else's business.

All of which (and there's more) might in fact render *Far From Heaven* open to a deeply ironic homophobic, or 'anti-gay', reading. This is, of course, the director adopting a stance, and one that might seem in keeping with the era, although Haynes has also said that 'reality can't be a criterion for judging the success or failure of a film, or its effect on you'. Yet while the friendship between Cathy and Raymond – a friendship that teeters, tremulously, on the verge of romance – is the stuff of walks in woodland glades and poetic quotation, cast in an almost Arthurian frame, Frank's little secret is

Cathy and the viewer are ushered from Dr Bowman's inner sanctum

something dirty, to be pursued in darkness and anonymity, confessed in a tearful breakdown (twice), 'treated' in private therapy sessions with Dr Bowman which are kept strictly off-limits to both Cathy ('What I discuss with this doctor is private. It's part of the thing') and the viewer.

There is a telling scene between Cathy and Frank after their visit to Dr Bowman's practice, and one that might in fact reveal something about Frank's true character. It is also, interestingly, the only time that anyone swears in *Far From Heaven*. As they leave Dr Bowman's building – their quandary counterpointed by a sun-dappled couple kissing on a bench opposite – Cathy is in her solicitous mode, but Frank snaps angrily, 'Look! I just want to get the whole fucking thing over with! Can you understand that?' Frank is in fact already beside himself with barely restrained rage on leaving Dr Bowman's office. He's quaking even as they take the lift down to the ground floor (Haynes has described this as Dennis Quaid refining the 'cardboard' acting of Rock Hudson in the Sirk films). The suspicious viewer may wonder if the 'fucking thing' Frank is talking about is his treatment, or his discomfort at being caught out. Events will suggest that it is probably the latter.

Frank connects with his anger in the only scene where someone swears

Five

' "Just beyond the fall from grace,
Behold that ever shining place".'

Raymond

This quote, which caused no little debate at the time of the release of *Far From Heaven*, turns out to be another of the tripwires that Haynes planted in the film to catch the unwary viewer. It is presented as a bona fide quote, both in terms of Raymond's (well, Dennis Haysbert's) enunciation – during his emotionally charged exchange with Cathy outside the Ritz cinema, where he pauses, as though the quote should be self-explanatory – and its physical appearance in Haynes's script. It is written in quotation marks in the original script, along with a diagonal slash to mark the line break in the rhyme. This first led me to ransack all the usual suspects in search of the 'original': the Bible, Shakespeare, Blake, Milton, Bunyan, the Romantics, a whole slew of North American poets, to no avail. It seems that the quote is intended to sum up Raymond's belief that it is possible 'That one person could reach out to another … Take an interest in another … And that maybe, for one fleeting instant, could manage to see beyond the surface – beyond the colour of things.'

In fact, as Haynes has admitted, he made the quote up himself, an artfully literary conceit worthy, at least in its execution if not content, of a Borges or Calvino. Perhaps the Blakeian intensity of the couplet should have made us suspicious about the purported authenticity of Raymond's poetic speech, but Haynes's admission should put us on guard that not everything said in *Far From Heaven* is necessarily what it seems. That Blakeian intensity, however contrived or faked, with its implication that disgrace might lead the way to paradise or liberation, is just one of the many profound speeches that Raymond is fed during *Far From Heaven*. Another is his observation to Cathy in the art gallery, as they admire a painting by Joan Miró, that abstract art is 'picking up where religious art left off ... trying to show you divinity'.

Raymond's ability to come up with these gems has proven a stumbling block for even the film's most ardent admirers. As with his Zen-like calm in the face of everyday acts of oppression, from casual verbal abuse in a coffee shop or on the street, to the attacks by his neighbours and the brutal stoning of his daughter by three white schoolboys, the intention seems to be to establish Raymond as a wellspring and font of a wisdom unknowable to those around him, even Cathy herself. At times, Haynes seems to be loading Raymond with buddhahood, if only to make the racist whites seem all the nastier. It is also true, of course, that historically the majority of African-American people during this period would have learned that the most pragmatic response to white racism was to keep your mouth shut, although this would change when they found their voice at Little Rock, Selma and Montgomery.

Here, however, the intention seems to be to portray Raymond as a heroic archetype, modelled perhaps on the likes of the African-American intellectual and NAACP co-founder W. E. B. Du Bois, or even Duke Ellington, both of whom used quiet dignity (and, it has to be said, not a little middle-class African-American hauteur) as a weapon against racism. Like his white counterpart in *All That Heaven Allows*, Ron Kirby, Raymond is projected as a pantheistic deity, at home in nature, suffused in the earth tones of Haynes's complex colour palette. Unlike the earlier Rock Hudson character, however, Raymond's skin colour lends a frisson of miscegenation, and there are at least two *Mandingo* moments in *Far From Heaven*: Raymond's first, menacing, appearance beyond Cathy's French windows, and their later visit to Eagan's restaurant, when gardener and mistress of the house dance together. Yet for all his earthy wisdom, Raymond is also the most intellectual character we meet in *Far From Heaven*, as far as we know the only one with a university degree, and almost certainly the only person in Hartford who can pronounce Joan Miró's surname properly. Keen-eyed viewers will have also spotted a reproduction Miró hanging on Frank's office wall, facing his desk, the site of his discovery in flagrante delicto with another man. Given that Cathy is also first seen in public with Raymond in front of a Miró, it is almost as though Haynes has roped in the hapless Catalan abstractionist as a leitmotif announcing acts of transgression in *Far From Heaven*.[17]

It would, again, be heresy against the conventions of the genre if the Wise Negro figure were to emerge at the end unscathed. When his African-American neighbours attack Raymond's house at night in seeming retaliation for consorting with a white woman, this isn't simply an early example of 'black-on-black' violence, but the sort of inverted self-loathing that writers such as Bruno Bettelheim and Primo Levi recorded among some Jews in the Nazi concentration camps. (It does not seem too extreme to suggest that, from Haynes's chosen perspective, 1950s North America was effectively a Fascist state as far as African-American citizens were concerned.) Yet despite the vicious attack on his daughter, and the loss of his gardening business, Raymond will emerge as the least damaged of the three central characters in *Far From Heaven*, and the only one with any realistic chance of rebuilding his life.

Six

'It just isn't plausible for me to be friends with you.'

Cathy

Cathy's comment to Raymond, mere moments before his 'fall from grace' speech, is perhaps the strangest passage of dialogue in a film noted for its use of fractured, stumbling speech, which some have seen as Haynes opting for realistic speech patterns rather than the overwrought constructions of Sirk and his contemporaries.

That 'plausible', especially, sticks in the mind. Its most commonplace usage today is taken to mean 'believable', although the *Complete Oxford English Dictionary* gifts it with these ambiguities:

Deserving applause, acceptable. Such as to be received with favour. Praiseworthy, laudable, commendable. Having an appearance or show of truth, reasonableness of worth, apparently acceptable or trustworthy (but often with an implication of mere appearance), fair-seeming, specious. Characterized by presenting specious arguments, etc; fair-spoken (with implications of deceit).

Like an earlier, minor, linguistic curio, when Cathy tells son David to 'wash his teeth', when surely the word 'brush' would be on the tip of the tongue of any dentally aware parent, that 'plausible' could be Haynes the scriptwriter deciding that Cathy should be tongue-tied in this moment of crisis, when both she and Raymond have independently decided to break off their friendship. Equally, the 'plausible' could be a Brechtian wink at the audience, with Cathy as a one-woman Greek chorus commenting on the narrative itself and her actions as an actor in Haynes's drama. Certainly, there are far more, er, plausible words ending in -ble that Cathy might have come up with: possible, workable, tenable, conscionable, for starters.

Just what did she mean by 'plausible'?

The inevitable question that 'plausible' invites is: plausible to whom? Her, him, her family, the good citizens of Hartford, us the audience? Or was Haynes perhaps also writing with his OED definition by his side, particularly that 'implications of deceit'?

Haynes's treatment of Cathy's character is the most complex of all the three main characters in *Far From Heaven*, marked – and troublingly so for this viewer – by his repeated comments when publicising the film on its release that she is an 'agent of control' in the film. Step back from the slow-motion train-wreck that devastates these lives, and you begin to wonder just how Cathy wields this agency, and what exactly she controls. She is, undoubtedly, in control of her home, and in a position of power in her community, but she is always under the aegis ('protection or sponsorship', according to the OED) of her husband, the sole wage-earner of the family (it's even ticked in a box on Frank's arrest sheet ...). Yet she is powerless either to help or alter her husband, and by brute circumstance alone unable to pursue the possibility of happiness with Raymond. As events unfold around her, entirely outside the influence of her own agency, we are left wondering if her position isn't just another convention of the genre: is Cathy the woman left holding together the centre that cannot hold, or merely someone shoring up a horrible fiction?

Haynes has always had an interesting interaction with women, both as collaborators and as characters. Quite clearly, he likes them, which cannot be said of all men – or, indeed, all homosexuals. His long-term collaboration with his producer Christine Vachon evidently goes beyond professional collaboration to a strong personal bond of friendship, and he has described Julianne Moore, only half-jokingly, as his 'muse'. Equally clearly, he sees them as complex, mutable characters, often bearing the brunt of pressures exerted by larger social agencies: the family, the institution of marriage, social and sexual conformity, body-image stereotypes, the normalising forces of peer pressure, consumerism, media, advertising, politics, and all the other ills of a society run largely by and for men.

His first post-university film, after the early student work
Assassins: A Film Concerning Rimbaud (1985), set the tone for
Haynes's unconventional representation of women in film: the
'underground' *succès de scandale Superstar: The Karen Carpenter
Story* (1987). Although never meant to become an underground
classic, it was propelled to that status when first the Carpenter family
and then toy manufacturers the Mattel Corporation complained, the
latter about the use of 'Barbie-like' dolls (actually just a jumble of
junk-store toy doll parts, but Mattel came after Haynes anyway) to
represent The Carpenters, their family and other characters.
Richard Carpenter finally won his 1990 injunction against Haynes's
early perverse masterpiece over the unlicensed use of Carpenters
songs in the soundtrack. What probably rankled most was the film's
portrayal of Karen Carpenter, dead of anorexia-induced heart failure
at the age of thirty-two, as a conflicted young woman willed into
fame and wealth by a scary family (her mother's first appearance in
Superstar bears an uncanny resemblance to Norman Bates's maternal
parent in *Psycho*). Richard Carpenter is himself implicated in this
melodrama attended by dark family shadows; at one point, 'Karen'
threatens 'Richard' during an argument, saying that she will tell their
parents about his 'private life', leaving the viewer to guess at what
exactly that might entail.

Haynes frames Karen Carpenter's slow demise with inserts of
charged images from the era: war atrocities, Richard Nixon on TV,
student riots, the blanket bombing of Vietnam and other
contemporary footage, suggesting that her death was a rather more
complex event than the death-by-Ex-Lax of a young woman who
thought she was fat. With its captioned and voiceover disquisitions on
anorexia, the food industry and its marketing tactics, Haynes's film
immerses Karen Carpenter into a media-saturated environment
reminiscent of Don DeLillo's early novel *White Noise*. It is, in fact, the
first in a number of films where Haynes enlists Susan Sontag's famous
notion of illness as metaphor, in which she saw it frequently misread
as a moral failing on the part of the unwell, the idea of illness as the

product of a character flaw, and one in which the ill are 'blamed' for their condition. It will reappear in the 'Horror' segment of his debut feature-length film, the triptych *Poison* (1991), and expand to fill the screen in his next, *[safe]*, his first film featuring Julianne Moore.

[safe] is his second film to focus on woman-in-extremis. The film was and remains titled in lower case and in parentheses. Those two humble punctuation marks literally surround it in a whirlwind of ambiguities: is *[safe]* ironic, implied, secret, revealed, 'irrelevant, spurious' (*OED*), comical, subversive or merely a pretty titles design conceit? It is set in similar terrain to *Far From Heaven*, suburban North America, although in the relatively recent setting of the late 1980s. Moore's character, Carol White, inhabits a modern-day equivalent of Cathy's dream home, except this one resembles the set of an ecological science-fiction thriller as it might be designed by Frank Lloyd-Wright. Carol begins to suffer a form of the much-contested 'total allergy syndrome', becoming allergic to the atmosphere, colours, smells, foodstuffs, even her favourite drink, milk. As her symptoms worsen, frustrating extensive allergy analyses and inviting the inevitable suggestions that her problems may be psychosomatic, Carol sequesters herself at a New Age healing centre in the New Mexico desert. Finally, she moves into a *[safe]* porcelain-lined igloo in its grounds, where we last see her telling herself 'I love you' again and again in a mirror.

In *[safe]*, Haynes effectively quarantines the viewer from any conventional narrative palliatives, beyond the steady progress of Carol's decline – a tactic that alienated some viewers and critics. He also refuses to offer any closure, leaving the viewer to wonder if Carol's allergy isn't, in fact, triggered by her husband, their relationship, their life, their milieu. Carol's self-immurement in the igloo is said to be part of her cure, but we are also left wondering, given the fate of its previous occupant, if it might not become her tomb.

For the first and so far only time in Haynes's films, here the spectre of AIDS makes a physical, explicitly named, appearance.

The founder of the desert healing centre, Peter, a single man of unspecified sexual orientation, 'has' AIDS, and once had a dream in which his hands were covered with what sound like Kaposi's sarcoma lesions, but these were transformed into beautiful flowers. Throughout his career, Haynes has resolutely refused to address AIDS directly, even though it might be said to stalk through most of his films, from *Poison* up to *Far From Heaven* and even *I'm Not There* (2007), which he has discussed in terms of identity as a form of 'infection'. (Is *Far From Heaven* an infection narrative? Conventionally, no, but when you consider the reaction of others to Cathy and Raymond's friendship – the ballet-school moms and daughters, the cinema queue, Mr Hey! Boy!, the diner busboys and clientele, the gallery visitors, in fact just about anybody who sees them together – then Cathy and Raymond could be living through one very long *Bodysnatchers* moment. Furthermore, it's about to happen to Frank, too, once his relationship with Blond Boy goes public.) AIDS remains the elephant in the room, and has variously been assigned the properties of allegory, allusion and metaphor by disputatious observers, but Haynes, given his contrary approach to narrative, would probably prefer that it remain an unnamed presence.

[safe] might in fact be seen as a bridging film between Karen in *Superstar* and Cathy in *Far From Heaven*, part of an unintended and hitherto unconsidered trilogy of woman-in-extremis narratives, and couched in Haynes's outspokenly pro-feminist (or perhaps post-feminist) worldview. All three women are, if not victims as such, then casualties in a far-ranging undeclared conflict in their society, a guerrilla engagement that encompasses gender, race, class, age, sexual orientation, wealth and status, and one that is acted out in small domestic and public/social spaces between individuals rather than by armies on battlefields. All three women are under the aegis of husbands, brothers, family. All three rebel, in different ways, against that aegis, although only Karen achieves a final conclusion, and she ends up dead on the bathroom floor. Cathy's predicament is by far

the most commonplace – it can be summed up by the film-poster epigraph, 'What imprisons desires of the heart?' – but Haynes's choice of what had previously been dismissed by some as a hackneyed genre if anything throws her dilemma into even sharper relief. The critique is there if you want to pick up on it, and in *Far From Heaven* and its ur-text, *All That Heaven Allows*, and other films by Sirk and his contemporaries, Haynes has found the perfect mount for the mirror in which he wants to reflect the world, although he himself is too busy, or perhaps too interested in, telling stories.

It is worthwhile considering Haynes's likely awareness of a key text on classic cinema melodrama, author and theorist Thomas Elsaesser's 1972 *Monogram* magazine essay, 'Tales of Sound and Fury: Observations on the Family Melodrama',[18] not least its identification of the domestic staircase as an almost religious site in the genre (it's there in *Far From Heaven*, when Ophüls's camera takes wing on the stairs in *The Reckless Moment*, and in most of Sirk and elsewhere besides). Haynes actually quotes Elsaesser's essay in his commentary to the DVD release of *Far From Heaven*, and no doubt it sits alongside Barthes, Lyotard and others on the bookshelves of his Portland house.

Elsaesser identified six factors that define melodrama: its use of music (from the classical Greek *melos*, melody, and *drama*, for, well, drama); the presence of social pressures; the inability of characters to act freely; characterisation and the use of stereotypes; the privileging of the victim's point of view; frequent variations between emotional extremes. Tracing the form as far back as the medieval morality play, Elsaesser characterises the twentieth-century cinematic version as a type of narrative whose template was stamped by post-Victorian conservatism and the theories of Sigmund Freud. Writing specifically about Sirk but also embracing the work of Ophüls, Ray, Minnelli, Cukor and others, Elsaesser offers a deft analysis of Sirk's characters that we should bear in mind when considering the behaviour of Cathy, Frank, Raymond and others in *Far From Heaven*. Their behaviour is often 'pathetically at variance with the real objectives they want to achieve'; they 'are never up to the demands which their lives make on them'; and, an observation likely to set the church bells ringing in Hartford, 'they take on suffering and moral anguish knowingly, as the just price for having glimpsed a better world and having failed to live up to it'. Harsh words, but Elsaesser lays the blame squarely on 'the impossible contradictions that have turned the American Dream into its proverbial nightmare'.[19] This, then, is the human condition that Haynes is examining in *Far From Heaven*.

We should also examine Haynes's use of and attitude to the family, not least in the light of his fascination with Freud and his famous essay, 'A Child Is Being Beaten',[20] which informs Haynes's thirty-minute television short *Dottie Gets Spanked* (1993) and also supplies a visual trope that recurs in both *Superstar* and *Poison*. Given Haynes's academic leanings, we might also expect it to come with a fair sprinkling of Michel Foucault's theories about sexuality, power and control, too.

The family is implicated as essentially flawed in most of Haynes's films (it's even there in reporter Arthur Stuart's dysfunctional childhood home in *Velvet Goldmine*). While Cathy and Frank have produced two children and share moments of tenderness, there is a spooky detachment to their actions, as though these are people going through the motions of how they think they ought to behave. (Originally, there were no children in Haynes's preparatory notes for *Far From Heaven*, which he envisioned as being set in the 'Fifties non-child-centric era'.) There is something particularly eerie about Cathy's family in *Far From Heaven* (and it is, unquestionably, Cathy's film); it is almost as though her family, like her home, is a domestic appliance that she hasn't quite got the hang of yet. Her husband's life, either when he is out at work or the few hours he spends at home, is an offshore realm that she is rarely, if ever, able or allowed to visit. As well as his ever-flexible work hours, there are vast tracts of her husband's life about which she knows nothing, either now or in that past when he 'had problems'.

In the few times when they are allowed to interrupt the adult spaces of the home, the children are rarely represented as anything more than an inconvenience; even in the 'happy' scene around the Christmas tree, Cathy brushes away Janice's request for help with her new ballet shoes with a polite 'In a minute, dear.' (There is also the mystery of their presence in the back seat in Cathy's final car journey in the film, to see Raymond off at the station. We are led to assume that she is leaving the house on her own for this poignant farewell; by the time she has got into the car, someone – Haynes, obviously – has planted the kids in the back, ready to complain 'Why are we pulling in here?' and 'Where are you going?' when she leaves them in the car at the station.) While Cathy is delighted that her daughter wants to grow up to be as beautiful as she is, the children are two Midwich Cuckoos whose main function is as a source of minor irritation. Indeed, if Cathy were able to realise her brief fantasy of fleeing to Baltimore with Raymond, Frank having already left home to 'be with' Blond Boy, the irksome offspring would be left alone in the house with only Sybil to look after them.

Sybil is the only true domestic partner Cathy has in the film, which as well as a nod to Sirk's *Imitation of Life* (1959) is also a reference to an earlier African-American stalwart, her namesake in Ophüls's *The Reckless Moment*. Despite the fact that Cathy's life appears to entail little more than the occasional shopping trip and the odd sports or ballet-school run (oh, and the weekly carpool), Sybil seems to shoulder most of the work around the house. Apart from her role as a telephonic sybil, she is also clearly a guardian angel figure, initially suspicious of Raymond out of her protectiveness towards Cathy, soldiering on with the polishing at the end when Cathy's life is shuddering to a halt. This is clearly an allusion to the interracial friendship between Lana Turner's Lora Meredith and Juanita Moore's Annie Johnson in *Imitation of Life*, where the struggling actress Lora takes in the homeless Annie, who subsequently becomes the heart and core of Lora's unconventional family. However, unlike the relationship between the white Lora and the black Annie, where friendship and familial love are presented as colour-blind, Cathy and Sybil are employer and employee in racially segregated Hartford, and that power balance only begins to modulate into friendship when Cathy's life is in ruins. Cathy only acknowledges her dependence on Sybil once: late on in the film, in the polishing scene prior to the trip to the station, she falteringly admits, 'I don't know how on Earth I'd ever manage ...', her voice trailing off into silence. Cathy is the only outspoken anti-racist we meet in *Far From Heaven*, yet Haynes wants us to see that at times even she is capable of doing little more than paying unthinking lip-service to the idea.

When considering Haynes's treatment of the family, I am reminded of Laurie Anderson's dryly sour epigrammatical song title, 'Born, Never Asked'. While Carol in *[safe]* has yet to have children, she is clearly already failing in her ascribed duties as a wife and future parent. When we first encounter her, in an opening scene, she is faking sexual pleasure to gratify her husband, although this is almost certainly a reference to a key scene in another of Haynes's all-time top ten, Chantal Akerman's extraordinary minimalist meditation on domestic alienation, *Jeanne Dielman, 23 Quai du commerce, 1080 Bruxelles* (1975). As in *Superstar*, the 'Hero' section of *Poison*, *Dottie Gets Spanked* and Arthur's backstory in *Velvet Goldmine*, the nuclear family unit is presented as the crucible for a whole array of unimaginable woes – even though Haynes himself seems to have grown up in a happy one. He has spoken at length about how his reading of Freud has exerted its influence in these films. In particular, he cites the sadomasochistic power shifts of Freud's essay 'A Child Is Being Beaten' (in which, put very simplistically, Freud argues that the act of being beaten also stands for being loved). We might imagine that Haynes also shares some of Foucault's opinions about how society constructs systems for 'normalising' or controlling sexuality. In *Far From Heaven*, where everyone seems to be following an imagined script of their lives, almost fearfully, in the hope that everything will come out right, the family as a construct is as flimsy as Haynes's sets, an assemblage, in Frank's words (albeit in a different context), of 'smoke and mirrors'.

Seven

Lights, camera, action

The equipment-free aspect of reality here [in film] has become the height of artifice; the sight of immediate reality has become an orchid in the land of technology.

Walter Benjamin, 'The Work of Art in the Age of Mechanical Reproduction', in *Illuminations* (New York: Harcourt Brace, 1968), p. 233

Anyone who has read Walter Benjamin's famous essay, which also discusses the nature of representation, will know that even writing in the 1930s Benjamin already had a lot to say about the nature of film and how it manipulates the viewer's response to what they see on screen: the mediating effect of the presence of the camera and the production process that carries the film as far as the cinema itself; the death not only of Roland Barthes's famous Author but also of authenticity itself; and the irrecuperable loss of the 'aura' of the original.

While Benjamin and others saw, or see, this tension between reality and artifice as a problem, conversely Todd Haynes regards it as an exciting new set of tools to play with, and revels in the potential for authorial mischief that they offer. While the 'surface' version of *Far From Heaven* appears to be a conventional tale of star-cross'd lovers, beneath that surface Haynes is subverting norms and expectations at almost every turn.

Lights

Ask anyone who has seen this film what initially struck them most and many will probably say the lighting and colour. Haynes deploys an array of devices (often very simple gels and filters) to achieve very specific effects that are often so subtle they pass unnoticed. Lighting effects frequently disagree with the time of day being represented on screen, and often emanate from improbable sources: for example, the lighting of Cathy's arrival at Raymond's house, and the use of colour on her figure in the closing scenes on the railway platform, which are as bizarre as anything that avant-garde dramatist Robert Wilson (*Einstein on the Beach*, *Deafman Glance*, *the CIVIL warS*, etc.) has ever devised for his lavish yet minimal theatre and film works.

Those gorgeous panoramas of autumnal leaves may look like Vermont, but in fact were, as we have seen, shot in New Jersey, albeit a New Jersey made a great deal tuftier by the work of the four 'greenspersons' identified in the end credits. Although Cathy and Frank's house exists, and most internal shots were made on sets, many of the outdoor location shots were also designed, almost perversely, to appear like sets. It almost represents a little detour through Eco's hyper-reality (Haynes actually uses the term himself), and perhaps even a kiss blown to the fantastic landscapes – such as the billowing sheets of plastic that stood in for the sea in his *Casanova* (1976) – of later Fellini. (Indeed, *Far From Heaven*'s own moonlit 'ocean' in the Miami scenes is, in fact, a cloth backdrop encrusted with sparkling rhinestones for the 'sea'.) Cathy's front garden, first seen early on when the children leave for school, resembles a miniature version of the Yellow Brick Road from *The Wizard of Oz* (1939), although the path appears to have been in situ when Haynes and his locations manager found the site. Even the abundant foliage of the woodland glade where she and Raymond share their most intimate thoughts takes on an almost surreal appearance. Look a little closer, however, and you will see that their miniature Walden Pond is in fact landscaped, with wide steps leading down to the water's edge, suggesting that their Eden is in fact some corner of a municipal park.

Proof of sorts that Haynes intended to subvert the conventions of realism can be found in his script notes for a scene that didn't make the final cut. This short bridging scene of what appears to have been a brief journey in Raymond's truck was meant to justify his trip out into the countryside, to deliver some shrubs to a ranch, and to transport him and Cathy to that sylvan glade and another racial epiphany for Cathy. Haynes's script notes for this lost scene called for the following effect: '[Throughout the following exteriors REAR-PROJECTED facsimiles succor the close-ups, but all "natural splendor" should shimmer with process.]' That 'shimmer with

Dennis does Rock, Julianne does Jane; a glimpse of the happiness they know they don't deserve

process', with its clear demand that even nature itself should be given a glossy make-over, rendering it, in Haynes's own phrase, 'hyper-real', could have been painted on a sign nailed over the door of the production design office for *Far From Heaven*. As Haynes told the *LA Weekly*, 'Those exterior scenes look more fake than anything we did on a set.'[21]

The one element that distinguishes *Far From Heaven* from the strident coloration of its period equivalents is its use of subdued

Yet even their sylvan glade is landscaped (note steps at left); and even here there is no escape from racism tones, itself a homage to Sirk. Haynes has confessed that the star colour is periwinkle blue, in autumn and winter shades, first seen as a Rothko-like abstract block projected against the stairs that Cathy walks down, then in Frank's descent into the maelstrom outside the Ritz cinema. It accompanies Frank as he moves from the brightness of the cinema marquee, past the kissing couple under a street lamp and, in lowering gloom, past a hooker on the street and into the darkness of the alleyway and the nameless queer dive next to the cinema. (Here, Haynes and Bernstein modulate the theme tune to a tense Philip Glass-like pulse.)

Haynes also admits, equally perversely, that most of the lighting effects (notably, the improbable angles and bizarre blue and orange hues of the art gallery sequence) are intentionally hyper-real. Conversely, he sometimes finds himself surprised by unadorned nature: the sunlight that falls on the kissing couple outside Dr Bowman's clinic was a real-time accident, as were the natural light effects in the garden and woods that transform Raymond into the pantheist figure he is meant to be (the woodland scene is, in Haynes's words, a 'rip-off' from *All That Heaven Allows*, with Rock again in Walden Pond mood).

One of the genres most often overlooked in any discussion of Haynes's work is science fiction, at least beyond the 'Horror' segment of *Poison* and the flying saucer that seems to deliver the baby Oscar Wilde to Earth at the beginning of *Velvet Goldmine*. *[safe]* is lit and coloured like an ecological disaster thriller, and the predominant colour is, of course, an antiseptic white, which some have read as connoting a racial subtext (Carol lives in a pristine 'white-flight' suburban enclave). In *Far From Heaven*, beyond the primary periwinkle blue and the colours assigned to the three main characters, the lighting is often penumbral, almost film-noirish. The colour coding Haynes ascribes to the three main characters – blues, greens, oranges and reds for Cathy, glowing earth colours for Raymond, button-up office-suit greys and blues or dress-down casual pastels for Frank – refers back to Sirk's own use of colour and the colour charts created for individual films by the Technicolor film corporation's own Color Advisory Service between the 1930s and the 50s.

Haynes is quite unironically faithful to the grammar of Sirk and the Color Advisory Service, although he uses counterpoint, discord and other 'musical' devices in a complex, almost symphonic structure sketched by critic Scott Higgins in his essay 'Orange and Blue, Desire and Loss: The Colour Score in *Far From Heaven*' (also in *The Cinema of Todd Haynes*). In certain scenes – Frank's arrival home after the office kiss, the slap sequence in their living room, and the pool scenes in the Miami shots – lighting and colour take on a science-fiction appearance. The first two are shot in dark velvety blues where something like UV lighting makes the whites flare. The last is shot through an acrid yellow pall suggestive of the aftermath of nuclear or environmental disaster, perhaps echoing the glare of the renovated print of Sirk's *Written on the Wind* (1956) released in the 1990s. These are by no means the only science-fiction moments in *Far From Heaven*, although again this might be a reference to the use of surreal lighting effects in *The Reckless Moment* (the key car journey scene in Ophüls's film is lit as if to resemble a hallucination).

While much of the lighting and colour is in direct reference to Sirk – Scott Higgins memorably commented that 'watching *Far From*

'Perhaps you could get me a little ice.' Frank steps over the line

Heaven is like stepping into a steady downpour of references'[22] –
Haynes both ratchets up the colour effect while also dimming it to a
sepulchral fade to black. He plays the colours against each other,
counterpointing warmth and cold, light and dark (and *Far From
Heaven* is a surprisingly dark film), sometimes switching colours
between characters – such as the final phone conversation between
Cathy (an icy blue) and Frank (shot in warm reds) – effectively
upping the ante on Sirk. Haynes further uses lighting and colour to
confound the viewer's expectations, of both time (although some
incongruities in lighting and time of day have been put down to
shooting on a tight schedule) and place (the gallery scenes, the ballet
school, the railway station, among others), as though reminding us of
the artifice at work on the screen and our complicity in that artifice.
Higgins allows Haynes this caveat: 'That he is working in a genre
already marked by a tendency toward stylistic hyperbole further
insulates *Far From Heaven*'s baroque quotations from becoming
distracting,' and ultimately concludes that 'the fact that *Far From
Heaven* approaches its goal *so nearly* must give us hope that self-
awareness need not mean the loss of sincerity' (my italics).[23]

Camera

Haynes is always fulsome in praising his collaborators, particularly
cinematographer Edward Lachman, designer Mark Friedberg, his
frequent editor, the late James Lyons, and costume designer Sandy
Powell, and numerous others besides. It is cinematographer
Lachman's work that the viewer notices most, and he brings an
impressive, and often very European, curriculum vitae to *Far From
Heaven*, including work with Bertolucci, Godard, Fassbinder,
Herzog, Schlöndorff and Wenders. Perhaps digging out his Brecht
(or Barthes) again, Haynes has revealed that he deliberately places
characters at the edge of the shot, so that 'they never own the frame'.
Haynes, Lachman and editor Lyons constructed the film as an
exercise in mimesis of the techniques of Sirk, but 'amped up', in
Haynes's tellingly rock 'n' roll phrase, to emphasise action and

character through flowing dolly shots and dramatic framing, with the camerawork sometimes saying what the characters themselves cannot. (At one point, a ceiling seen from a certain angle becomes, in Haynes's words, 'the weight of bourgeois space' weighing down on Cathy.)

While Haynes may nudge individuals to the edge of the frame, double-headers and ensemble shots are conventionally geometrical, often symmetrical, although he sometimes manhandles camera angles to skew the characters' authority in certain takes. The opening and closing crane shots (requiring a ninety-foot crane camera) may allude back to *All That Heaven Allows*, but Haynes peppers them throughout the film, often quite exquisitely (Cathy's pursuit of her runaway scarf), and usually to give the viewer a superior knowledge of events occurring at ground level. At moments of tension (usually when the lighting turns blue), Haynes kilters the camera at something approaching forty-five degrees, recalling the crazy yawing camera angles of *The Third Man* (1949), while there are numerous reaction shots which he shoots from the ground up, the looming figures making characters or passers-by resemble extras from *Invasion of the Bodysnatchers* (1956). He even uses this device in the art gallery sequence, and in scenes between Cathy and Eleanor.

Shot from the ground up for that special *Bodysnatchers* effect

Beyond the conventional over-the-shoulder shot in face-to-face scenes, he also plays with camera angles from above and below eye-level, as if rewriting the grammar of who is allowed authority in these scenes, sometimes even pushing characters out of focus as if to diminish their status. In one notable scene between Cathy and Raymond that takes place in her garden, Haynes films them in a way that dwarfs Cathy as twice she faces Raymond, making him appear like a giant, an effect loaded with narrative ambiguity. But beyond some beautiful tracking shots – one following Cathy through the walls of her home, another accompanying her to a café to meet Raymond, which, in a further echo of Edward Hopper's work, resembles his famous 1942 painting *Nighthawks* as it might have been seen from behind the counter (and which also ends in another *Bodysnatchers* moment, that menacing '*Is there something I can do for you folks?*') – much of the main action takes place in cars.

Action

Todd Haynes loves cars almost as much as he loves women. From *Superstar* to *I'm Not There*, the opening credits sequence is barely over before one appears or you are bundled into the passenger seat of another by the camera. In both of those films, the car sequence is an establishing drive-by shot, and in both cases the point of view is one of surveillance, as though the camera is filming a crime scene (which, in the first film, it quite possibly is). In *[safe]*, we are actually driven *into* the film by a car (in fact, an allusion to Fassbinder's *Chinese Roulette* [1976]), and the automobile will take on the dual and contradictory roles of safe-room (as Carol's means of negotiating her alien and alienating landscape), but also as monster (contributing to the pollution that might be causing her illness, and at one point surprising her while she is out walking in the desert, threatening her in the manner of the tanker from *Duel* [1971]).

Far From Heaven is topped-and-tailed by car journeys, although the first is also a deliberate quote from *All That Heaven Allows*, as is the colour of Cathy's blue-and-white estate car, and the crane shot that introduces it. While automobile symbolism in film is nothing new – Barthes may have got it wrong about the car being 'the cathedral of the future', but it is a tireless signifier of status, wealth, mobility, sexuality and more – here the car becomes an extension of the home and, as often as not, the set on which some of the key dramatic moments are played out.

Cathy and Frank first discuss what 'really' happened the night he was arrested for 'loitering' while she drives him home from the police station in her car (there is an abiding mystery about Frank's own car, which I will address shortly). Raymond's garden business truck is the chariot that delivers Cathy to her woodland epiphany and, after that, to the sexually charged *Mandingo* moment when she and Raymond dance at Eagan's (here, Bernstein hands the house band a post-bop-era jazz arrangement of one of his themes). It is Cathy's appearance in Raymond's chariot that alerts the town gossip Mona Lauder (Celia Weston as a spiteful battleaxe in a hat with a net veil) to Cathy's implausible relationship with Raymond. Mona spots Cathy when she is collecting *her* car from an African-American carhop at a carwash in Hartford's African-American ghetto (leaving the mindful viewer to wonder why a woman like Mona Lauder would leave her car in the hands of a Negro, and in Hartford's answer to

Banished from the agora, Hartford-style

Harlem). It is also Cathy's car that will deliver her and witless daughter Janice to the ballet-school performance where Cathy's ostracism from Hartford society – and this is a real, banished-from-the-Greek-agora ostracism – is confirmed when the other ballet-school mothers and their daughters glare at them in undisguised contempt. And it is also a car that effects the several appearances by 'best friend' Eleanor to bear witness to various dramatic moments in the narrative.

Eleanor spots Cathy's bruise under her new hairdo; are we alone in suspecting Eleanor may be enjoying this?

Like Carol's car in *[safe]*, the automobile is of course the natural mode of travel in a culture where public transport is something that only poor people use, and equally obviously Haynes employs the automobile to get his characters to different sites of action. While they are common narrative devices, these car journeys become noteworthy when we consider that Haynes spends the later part of his narrative actively obscuring several journeys that Frank and his mystery car must undertake for the film to reach its predestined conclusion. In fact, these unseen car journeys will take Frank into a secondary secret love story that happens off screen, almost an entirely new movie, as though he has slipped into a parallel universe. Back in this one, the only person we see walking any significant distance is Raymond's daughter, Sarah, and she walks straight into trouble, to be baited, pursued and finally (and biblically) stoned by the three white schoolboys.

Frank's car is a mystery because we never actually see it, although it is clear from the 'I do feel able to locate my own car' scene that he does indeed own one. We never see it parked in the driveway of their house, nor do we ever see Frank driving it, although it is pressed into a kind of mute perjury when Cathy lies about a fictitious car accident to explain their absence from the dinner party the night Frank was arrested ('The car's fine,' she tells Eleanor on the phone when they get home from the police station. 'Frank says it was the bumper that got hit, but you know me. I can't tell the difference'). If Frank was out and about in his car the night he was arrested, he and Cathy are blissfully unconcerned about either its whereabouts or its safety as they drive home in her car. Nor are they particularly bothered about discussing its retrieval from where Frank may or may not have left it. Yet such is the strange magic of Frank's car that it led one reviewer (Andrew O'Hehir at *Salon*), when summarising the events of his fateful encounter with 'that snivelling junior cop', to claim that Frank's arrest was due to a 'fender-bender', when in fact he was arrested for, well, being a bender.[24]

Frank's car is just one of the many elisions in Haynes's narrative (Frank's passionate off-screen whirlwind romance with 'Blond Boy' is another, as is the unseen train of events that delivers him to Dr Bowman's office). It serves the dramatic requirements of Haynes's script, while at the same time withholding vital evidence from the viewer, almost in the manner of classic film noir, or the impossible narrative conundrums of, say, Peter Greenaway, Michael Haneke, Abbas Kiarostami or Alain Resnais.

Neither are we told anything more of Frank's encounter with that snivelling junior cop. Cathy has to sign something resembling a report or arrest sheet at the police station (indiscernible even in freeze-frame as she tosses it carelessly into the wastepaper basket at home), and she also receives a 'receipt', suggesting that she either paid bail or a spot fine for Frank. Whatever it was she threw into the wastepaper basket, where it would surely have been seen by Sybil – and it clearly contained at least seven lines of closely typed notes detailing Frank's suspicious behaviour – the authorities do not follow up their encounter with Frank. (But, then again, the cops never found out who killed Sean Regan in *The Big Sleep* [1946], either.)

With the exception of the rear projection borrowed from *All That Heaven Allows* when Cathy drives past Raymond's garden centre, the projections seen from the rear and side windows of her car are, of course, a knowing 'antiquing' effect in a film that could just as

The rear projection as postmodern 'antiquing' device

easily have used other modern devices, such as blue-screen morphing or a simple bonnet or dashboard-mounted camera. Instead, Haynes chooses to use – in fact fake – the technology that Sirk would have employed half a century earlier. The only one truly jarring switch between reality and artifice and back again occurs during Cathy's car journey to the station at the end of the film. She drives through a real street, but then gets out of the car against a comically obvious theatre-flat backdrop, before walking off through a real-life railway station. Whatever the reason for these journeys – to get Cathy to and from the police station, Raymond's business, the ballet school, the railway station or to Raymond's home – their main function is to take Cathy back to the central set in the film, her home.

While the exterior for the house was discovered in Ho-Ho-Kus, New Jersey – a large, Dutch-style gable-roofed suburban-modern mini-mansion with an unfenced front lawn and a backyard giving onto woodland, the sort of property that wouldn't look amiss in *Little Women* or *Mr Blandings Builds His Dream House* (or *Perfect Housewives* or *Brothers and Sisters*, come to that) – the interiors were constructed on a series of cutaway sets on a temporary sound stage built at a former military base in nearby Bayonne. Yet the discrete spaces – Cathy and Frank's bedroom, the stairwell, lounge, kitchen and family room, dining and breakfast rooms, and the various ingresses and egresses to front and back gardens – are so eerily unattached to each other that it would be virtually impossible to draw a schematic diagram of the house from memory. Their house also seems to extend far beyond the spaces that we are allowed into by the camera, or indeed the spaces used by the family, implying a vast area of unused space beyond those rooms clustered around the stairwell, which, as Thomas Elsaesser pointed out, is never just a set of stairs but, rather, a theatrical space reserved for moments of high drama.

Cathy and Frank's house is built around the camera, constructed on different levels that give characters (notably in the party sequence) authority as they move around the set, allowing elevation for camera angles, but at other times forcing characters to take meaningless hikes up and down split-level areas. From the plans for the sets, what we see of the interior was organised down to the last split-level stair and sunken seating area to cram each shot with unspoken meaning (meaning, in fact, as Elsaesser also points out, is typically displaced onto inanimate objects in most cinematic melodrama). Like the carefully enhanced woodland scenes, these hyper-real interiors are spaces dreamed up like images snipped from lifestyle magazines and assembled in collage form, which appears to have been the way Haynes storyboarded the film. This only serves to introduce another level or layer of mediation, making it a film constructed from the director's interpretations of fictions snipped from other media, in effect piling on the artifice.

Frank's office is also a curio, and not just for the oddly post-dated electric typewriters in its typing pool. The very siting of Magnatech's office is itself an oddity. Why would a major television manufacturing company have its offices in the boondocks of Connecticut rather than a tall steel-and-glass skyscraper somewhere like Chicago or New York? The answer is revealed when Frank's colleague Stan Fine (Michael Gaston) mentions at one point that 'New York have just shaved a week off portfolio season', and Haynes's script notes make reference to the two men working in the 'Hartford division' of Magnatech, implying that the Corporation has a New York, possibly Manhattan, headquarters. Either Frank and Stan have yet to make it up the career ladder to 'New York', or, and this is more likely, a fictionalised suburban 'Hartford' presented Haynes with the ideal group of neighbouring locales in which to set his characters moving, and perhaps for reasons not too dissimilar to those behind a film such as *The Truman Show* (1998).

The idea of an entire town approached as a film set also allows Haynes to erect and dissolve barriers across which his characters can commit various acts of trespass or transgression, and with witnesses ever to hand. The barriers – of race, class, sexuality, social status, conformity and transgression – are mobile, and often invisible, moved around at the whim of the Hartford boundary commissioner, one Todd Haynes. The barriers are in fact arbitrary, there to be interpreted according to prejudice – what might seem a harmless chat with the gardener to one person is a furtive act of adultery to another – the small-town setting only intensifying the impression that everyone in Hartford-qua-America is under surveillance by everybody else.

Perhaps for budgetary reasons, in Frank's rather anonymous Hartford office setting, where daylight never shows through permanently closed curtains, nowhere are there the Men Standing Around in Tall Glass Skyscrapers that we might remember from *Written on the Wind*, or indeed, contemporary television's *Mad Men*. *Mad Men*, in fact, while produced for an entirely different medium, might offer an interesting mirror-image to the milieu and era that Haynes evokes here. It is set (or began) in 1960, just two years after *Far From Heaven*, and in a Manhattan ad agency that might conceivably have pitched for the Magnatech portfolio if it were out for tender. *Mad Men*'s lead character, Don Draper (Jon Hamm), also leads a Town-and-Country double life, serially cheating on his wife in Manhattan while she languishes, in what might in fact be a roundabout allusion to *Far From Heaven* itself, in a similar exurban modern dream home in Ossining, upstate New York.

While *Mad Men*'s ultra-competitive admen chain-smoke, take three-martini lunches, do drugs and listen to *Kind of Blue* while having sex with their mistresses, Frank, Stan and their circle are, if only because of the requirements of Haynes's script, their unsophisticated country cousins. Simple logistics alone insist that *Far From Heaven* could not play in the glass canyons of mid-town Manhattan.

Beyond her few forays outdoors, Cathy's life is largely circumscribed by the perimeter of her home, and it is likely that Haynes wants us to see her as suffering from a genteel form of domestic imprisonment almost as pernicious as Carol's in *[safe]*. The very first evening of the film's timeframe, we watch as she prepares herself at her triple-sided vanity mirror above a dressing table decked with perfumes, creams and other beauty products, watched by adoring daughter Janice ('When I grow up, will I look like you?'). When Frank doesn't show up in time for their dinner date, it is evident even before the call from the police station that it would be unthinkable for Cathy to go to the dinner party on her own in a town and a culture like Hartford – or, indeed, Anywhere, USA, in this era. She exists chiefly as a cipher for Frank's success, representing all that the *Hartford Weekly Gazette* tells its readers is exemplary about the ideal modern American housewife and homemaker – which is precisely why the newspaper wants to interview her. Sometimes, she merely exists simply as a cipher for Frank himself: the officer on the phone from the police station addresses her as 'Mrs Frank Whitaker'.

Apart from errands and chores, she leaves the house for purely personal reasons just twice in the entire film, and both adventures end in trouble. The first outing is to the art gallery, where she is surprised to see Raymond, explaining the wonders of Abstract Expressionism to his daughter Sarah. Haynes also uses the gallery scene, mischievously, to introduce another unlovable homo, the vile snob art dealer Morris Farnsworth (J. B. Adams). Farnsworth's character is written as a shameless appeal to the viewer's instinctive dislike of everything he is designed to represent. He may be intended to offer a contrast to Raymond's intuitive appreciation of art, but the scene overwhelmingly confirms the impression that the homosexuals in Haynes's film are the sort that the modern homo would cross the street to avoid. (Farnsworth had a larger role in the original script, which elaborated his character and the difference between one side of Hartford and the other, but Haynes decided to cut it.)

The scene is key, however, in establishing a public friendship between the white woman and the African-American man; before it is over, tongues are already wagging ('Who is that man?' Eleanor asks. 'You have the whole place in a clamour!'). It is also the second reminder that Cathy is under surveillance by the press camera, whose flashbulb explodes in her face again when she is 'communing with Picasso', to quote the society editor Mrs Leacock (Bette Henritze).

Mrs Leacock's article will also record that Cathy is 'kind to Negroes', a quote that will not go unnoticed in Hartford society, and will in fact be used as secondary evidence against her.

The second outing occurs when she relents and accepts Raymond's offer of a drive in the countryside. After their Walden Pond moment with the sprig of flowering witch-hazel, and their daring visit to Eagan's bar and diner, she and Raymond again fall under surveillance, this time by Mona Lauder, who now clearly believes she has enough evidence to convict (as, alas, will the rest of white Hartford).

Apart from the daytime pyjama-party scene, when a group of friends converge on Cathy's house for an afternoon of daiquiris and gossip – but not before a gust from a handy passing wind machine has blown Cathy's scarf over the house into the garden, where it will be retrieved by Raymond, leading to another Arthurian moment between them – Cathy is effectively a solitary prisoner in her dream home. Her relationship with her children is best described as testy, and no one in this family – or, indeed, in Hartford, apart from the African-Americans – seems to go to church. Her only contact with the outside world is either the odd shopping errand or to social events in the company of Frank, who, either because of pressure of work or

Eleanor (left) leads her troupe in a round of daiquiris and disclosures

simple avoidance, is often too busy to attend even these. Yet until she meets Raymond, and until Frank's true nature is revealed, Cathy seems more than content with her life, effectively walled up like an anchorite in a prison fitted out with the latest time-saving domestic gadgets and (like Carol's teal-coloured sofa in *[safe]*) thoroughly modern interior décor.

The afternoon daiquiri-party scene, where Sandy Powell conducts a symphony of pinks and reds on Cathy's Yellow Brick

Sandy Powell's symphony of reds and the scarf that got away

Road, is also intended to reveal other control systems at work in Hartford. As head girl, Eleanor leads her troupe in a giggling discussion of their husbands' sexual demands. Sex for these women is a disagreeable domestic chore, and something they would clearly prefer to do without. The first reveals that her husband insists on sex at least once a week, the second, two or three. Eleanor, while remaining reticent about her own sex life, regales them with a friend's report of a husband who demands sex daily, and twice daily at weekends. Cathy herself also demurs, smiling embarrassedly, but Haynes saves her any further discomfort by abruptly cutting the scene, leaving us both none the wiser about her sex life with Frank but also reminded of the fact that their marital bed is not a happy one. (Later, Frank will in effect attempt to rape her on the sofa, as she lies back supine, pretending to respond, almost as though echoing Carol's behaviour in the sex scene that opens [safe], not to mention the surprise that awaits the viewer at the end of Akerman's *Jeanne Dielman*).

If there is a monster loose on this Forbidden Planet, it is the telephone. It is one of a trio of mechanical devices – phone, press camera, TV – that harbour baleful intent. It also rings, literally and metaphorically, the changes as Haynes's narrative unfolds.

Rule Number One chez Cathy and Frank is: if the phone rings, *duck!* As it will only be bad news (what's Frank done *now*? Which local gossip is bad-mouthing Cathy today?), it is usually handled by Cathy or Sybil. Academic and critic Lynne Joyrich, in her essay 'Written on the Screen: Mediation and Immersion in *Far From Heaven*' (also from the *Camera Obscura* collection *A Magnificent Obsession*), identifies eight significant telephone calls (in fact, there are eleven all told, including a tantalising call left unanswered as Cathy hurries out of the house) that punctuate and propel the narrative, and in a way that 'almost functions itself as a musical score, composed in a sequence that forms a rhyming structure'.[25]

These phone calls begin with the one Cathy receives from Hartford police station, asking her to collect Frank – Joyrich reads this as 'Frank being put into Cathy's custodial care (in effect, under "house arrest")'.[26] This is followed by a scene where Frank asks his secretary to call Cathy so that he can tell her he will be 'working late' again, when in fact he plans to go out cruising. The third call, some days later, is also from Frank, who is calling Cathy to apologise that he is again working late. This inspires Cathy to take him some dinner, with the calamitous results we have already seen. The next is a call from a friend releasing Cathy from carpool duty and enabling her to accept Raymond's no less fateful invitation to go for a drive, where they end up in that sylvan glade, Raymond the unlikely Lancelot to Cathy's Guinevere.

By the next afternoon, 'best friend' Eleanor is on the phone to report that Mona Lauder's telephone tree is ringing off the hook: 'It's Mona, Cathy. She's – well, she's just been on some kind of rampage, swearing she saw you and a coloured man, somewhere out on Franklin, coming out of a truck.' Panicked, Cathy lies about her afternoon with Raymond ('The entire thing is so absurd!'), but before she can finish her phone conversation with Eleanor, Frank arrives home early from work, drunk and in a mean mood.

Apparently, Mona Lauder's telephone tree has reached the creative department of Magnatech. 'Christ, Cathleen!' he bellows. 'Do you

Never lie to a telephone …

even have the slightest idea what this means? Do you realise the kind of effect this could have on me and the reputation I've spent the past eight years of my life trying to build? For you and the children and the company?' Clearly, Cathy's normally peaceable mode won't mend things here, and when she tries to defend herself against Mona's gossiping, Frank snaps, 'Please! Spare me the Negro rights!' This forces Cathy to lie yet again, declaring that she has already sacked Raymond, when she hasn't.

The inanimate Bakelite object sitting on the hallway occasional table here reveals its true monstrous powers: it has contrived to have Frank suspended from his job, what he sourly calls 'sort of an early Christmas bonus ... a month of rest and relaxation'. In truth, he has been sidelined during Magnatech's busiest period of the year, when he should be masterminding the corporation's new marketing campaign. Instead, he has been put out to pasture because of his wife's seeming crime against white propriety, and with ominous implications for his career prospects. This will lead to Cathy's 'plausible' speech to Raymond outside the Ritz cinema, and later to the Whitakers' equally fateful decision to take a holiday in Miami over the New Year.

Later, perhaps in guilt at having broken off her friendship with Raymond (at a meeting arranged by telephone, in a conversation that

... especially if Eleanor is on the other end

does not appear in Lynne Joyrich's list of calls), and also appalled at news of a violent racist attack in the town (but unaware as yet that the victim was Raymond's daughter), Cathy rather sheepishly calls the NAACP to enquire about volunteering, only for the call to be interrupted by Frank's return home. Inexplicably, Frank bursts into tears, sending the distraught children running to their rooms, and finally breaks down and confesses to Cathy: 'I've fallen in love with someone – who wants to be with me.' (Perhaps prompting some viewers to wonder, 'And Cathy *doesn't*?') Cathy replies, either coolly or in a state of shock, 'I assume, then ... you'll be wanting a divorce?' Her surprising candour can only really be explained in terms of Haynes's citing of both Sirk and Elsaesser on the improbable, or self-defeating, behaviour of the classic melodramatic heroine archetype.

The telephone still isn't quite finished with Cathy. It will help her to arrange a meeting with 'best friend' Eleanor, where Eleanor will turn on Cathy and side with Mona Lauder. And finally, it will trill one last time when Frank calls from his hotel room for that spookily cheery chat about their divorce plans, while Blond Boy lounges on the bed behind him.

Considered as a *deus ex machina*, the telephone plays such a large part in the narrative of *Far From Heaven* that by rights it ought to have its own place in the cast credits. In a film set some decades before surveillance technology became either a civil rights issue or the stuff of cinematic paranoia narratives, it places Cathy in a network where information, specifically personal secrets, begins to move around of its own accord. Compared to the telephone, the press camera is merely an annoyance, although one that has already displayed its ability to enter Cathy's house without either her permission or indeed her knowledge, until it is literally in her face. The television, while a largely benign window on the outside world, usually off limits to the children and used by Frank as either background distraction or an escape mechanism when he tries to avoid a difficult conversation with Cathy, also sits in the family room as a harbinger, if not of doom, then of unavoidable and

uncomfortable change. There is also a television in the master bedroom, but that was wheeled in by the director himself to let Frank watch Eisenhower talking about Little Rock on the news and for Haynes to connect a video feed from the wider racial drama unfolding in the world outside the house. The bussing that Eisenhower announces will take place in Little Rock will have a knock-on effect in Selma and Montgomery, but its repercussions will also reach Hartford, the place where partygoers still think 'there are no blacks'.

Eight

'Miami! Everything's pink!'

Cathy

Before the telephone rings for the last time, Haynes seems to allow his characters, and his audience, one last shot at redemption. Here, again, we should be forewarned that all may not be what it seems. Haynes has confessed on numerous occasions that he likes Sirk's idea of the trick 'impossible' happy ending; thus those white

Eisenhower appears on Haynes's handy bedroom video feed, anchoring indoor dramas to those outside

spring blossoms in the closing crane shot may seem symbolic of rebirth but are probably also booby-trapped. Is the trip to Miami really a chance for Cathy and Frank to give their marriage another go or, following another convention of the genre, the director-writer merely piling on more agony?

Even though three lives – at least – are mangled in Haynes's narrative train-wreck, the director-writer still allows his characters some humour, if tinged with a hint of the gallows. On Christmas morning, Cathy interrupts Frank's first drink of the day with an extra, surprise, present: a gift-wrapped box containing brochures for Acapulco, Cuba, Mexico, Rio, Miami and Bermuda. Frank suggests maybe Miami (but, oddly, passes over Cuba and Mexico entirely). 'Miami!' Cathy gasps. 'Everything's pink!' 'Oh, really?' says Frank, comically grim. 'Hmmmm. Maybe we should consider Bermuda …'

Their amusement is no doubt shared by the director and his cast and crew, and anyone who suspects they may have heard muffled laughter from behind the camera will find that they are not alone: Haynes has admitted to 'giggling' at parts of *Far From Heaven* himself. The 'pink' joke is part of a seam of 'gay' referentiality in *Far From Heaven*. Beyond its (also arguable) interpretation as camp, *Far From Heaven* asks us the blunt question: Is this queer, post-queer,

Cathy interrupts Frank's first drink on Christmas morning

none-of-the-above? Is it a volte-face by the director of *Poison*, or a Trojan horse left overnight on the red carpet at the Academy Awards? And who is co-opting whom here? I will be exploring *Far From Heaven*'s queerness shortly.

Pink architecture or no, Cathy and Frank plump for Miami, as a break for Frank, a little treat for themselves after all that they have been through, and the chance to put a little romance back into their lives. For Cathy, it is possibly her first holiday in many years: the last one mentioned is a trip to Vermont, 'before Janice was born'. Given that Janice is played by the (then) ten-year-old Lindsay Andretta, this only adds to the suspicion that Cathy has been willingly walled up in her perfect home for the best part of a decade, a 'perfect prisoner', as James Mason calls Joan Bennett in *The Reckless Moment*.

Within the space of a split-second jumpcut, we are on the terrace of a hotel in Miami, rhinestones spangling on that Felliniesque 'ocean', and Cathy and Frank are dancing as the clock counts down to midnight on New Year's Eve. Frank is 'gussied up' in white tux and bow tie, while Cathy wears another of Sandy Powell's knockout frocks. As the happy couple return to their table, the house band playing a cha-cha arrangement of Elmer Bernstein's theme tune, they pass a family being seated at their own table. Frank makes eye

A surprise present that everyone will live to regret

contact with one of the sons, who will turn out to be Blond Boy, aka Kenny, although right now he might just as well be Tadzio from Visconti's *Death in Venice* (1971). Frank actually makes eye contact with the 'boy' twice, which in cruising body language is tantamount to foreplay, and this mere minutes before he and Cathy are waltzing under the stars (no, 'stars') and wishing each other a happy New Year. Perhaps borrowing the phrase from the 1932 Ernst Lubitsch romantic comedy, this is probably what Haynes has referred to as the theme of 'trouble in paradise' in *Far From Heaven*.

The next day, despite lighting effects that might suggest they have been transported to the surface of Venus, Frank and Cathy are luxuriating by the pool. As though reminding us of the reason why we're here, Haynes inserts the race card again, as a little African-American boy runs up and jumps into the pool, effectively contaminating it. Before his father, a waiter at the hotel pool bar, can pull the boy out and scold him, the whites have already started clambering out of the water, another crane shot revealing the pool to be spookily empty in that strange marine Miami light. Cathy and Frank are merely bemused (even Haynes's script says that Frank merely 'shrugs'), despite Cathy's earlier claim that they support equal rights for the Negro. She is more concerned about the whereabouts of

Frank clocks Kenny, although right now his name might as well be Tadzio

Cathy and Frank, poolside and happy before the storm; her *Cosmo* finished, it's time for Cathy's 'Miz Mitchell', and Frank's first encounter with Kenny; the marine light of Miami and that deserted pool

her holiday read, 'my Miz Mitchell' (presumably Margaret, author of *Gone with the Wind*), which she has inadvertently left in their room. In a trice, Frank is off to fetch it for her.

Here, the sceptical viewer is expected to make a number of leaps of the imagination that somehow deliver Blond Boy, who has spied Frank across the pool, to the door of the hotel room as Frank returns to collect Cathy's book. Curiously, Frank – well, Todd Haynes actually – also does something that few sensible hotel guests ever do: he leaves the door wide open as Frank rummages in their hotel room for Cathy's 'Miz Mitchell'. This enables him to see, as we do, Blond Boy standing in the doorway, reflected in a mirror, bathrobe undone, fingertips teasingly stroking his chest and dawdling down towards his belly button (the script originally had his fingers 'quietly grazing his crotch'). 'Slowly,' says the script, 'like a sleepwalker, Frank begins to approach, music deepening. FADE TO BLACK.' As in almost every film of the genre and era, the bedroom door swings shut on us as the camera approaches it.

We never see what does or does not happen between Frank and Blond Boy in the hotel room, nor even if Cathy gets to finish her 'Miz Mitchell', because the scene actually fades back to Hartford, and to Sarah, who is being pursued by the three white schoolboys, led by 'Hutch' (Kyle Smyth), David's best friend. In the very next scene, the kids are welcoming Cathy and Frank home, David has something he wants to tell his dad, and there's the devil to pay for what's been going on since they went away.

Nine

'What on Earth has gotten into this town?'

Cathy

Whatever transpired in Miami – and it will take a quantum leap in events to take Frank from that hotel room doorway to the next scene in which we encounter him – by the time Cathy and Frank return home, the scene is set for the denouement of the two narrative arcs of the film.

David's news is that Hutch and two boys have been expelled from school for 'throwing a rock at a girl'. Frank corrects him: 'You mean "suspended".' 'No!' David insists. 'Expelled! I swear!' 'That's *terrible*,' Cathy says, adding, 'You mean a little girl from school?' To which David replies, with a telling non sequitur, 'No. She was a Negro,' which is a curious semantic construction, because Sarah was on her way home from *a* school when Hutch and the other boys, seemingly from the same school, attacked her. Moreover, the boys clearly know her and the circumstances of her father's friendship with Cathy (Hutch, the ringleader, goads her about her 'daddy' and 'daddy's white girlfriend'). The possibility that the two families know each other, either from school or work, is pointedly reinforced in the art gallery scene when Raymond reminds Sarah of the time they visited the Hutchinsons at home, implying some form of social contact between them.

In fact, between script and final cut, several scenes have been rearranged here. In the script version, the attack on Sarah occurs prior to the Christmas Day scene in the Whitaker household. In the final cut, it takes place immediately after the Miami sequence. In both, however, Sarah is identified as a student at David and Hutch's school. Mere geography alone would suggest that she is returning home from the same place. Moreover, Hutch and his friends must know her and something of her family circumstances to give meaning to their pursuit and brutal attack.

In the original script, David is among the group of boys who are about to pursue Sarah after school, but he is plucked from the scene by the surprise arrival of Cathy in her car. This scene does not appear in the final cut. It is very probably little more than one of the exigencies of editing, and either version of the sequence of events would still lead us to David's telling statement that she is just 'a Negro'. Perhaps Haynes's intention here is to present David as a

Just teaching her a lesson. Hutch and friends explain the facts of life to Raymond's daughter, Sarah

young boy already versed in the casual, careless racism of Hartford, for he goes on to defend Sarah's attackers by saying, 'Hutch said they were just trying to teach her a lesson,' as though a savage stoning can be condoned or even construed as a 'lesson' about anything. Its chief intent, however, is to set Cathy up for a nasty surprise. Still unaware that Sarah was the victim of the attack, Cathy comments rhetorically, 'What on Earth has gotten into this town?' and, faced with no response from the rest of the household, collects the post that has arrived during their absence and takes it upstairs. It will be a full fortnight before Sybil finds the courage to tell Cathy that the victim in the attack was Sarah. By which time, Cathy's world will be coming apart at the seams.

However incongruously David's comment sits as a component in the narrative engine of Haynes's film – and beyond getting characters from situation A to situation B, the statement remains a bald denial of observable fact – it does serve to highlight the genteel apartheid of Hartford. Even Cathy, despite her noted kindness to Negroes, can slip into it as a default mode: witness the moment when she asks Sybil to deal with the NAACP people on the front doorstep, and her expression of mere bafflement when she looks up from her copy of *Cosmopolitan* to watch the little African-American boy being snatched from the pool by his father. The post she collected on their return from Miami included a leaflet from the NAACP, yet she still takes a fortnight to read it. When she finally phones to enquire about volunteering for the organisation, Frank arrives home with terrible news.

Ten

The double-edged potential for injury in the scene of gay coming out ...
results partly from the fact that the erotic identity of the person who receives the disclosure is apt also to be implicated in [it], hence perturbed by it.

Eve Kosofsky Sedgwick, *Epistemology of the Closet* (Berkeley: University of California Press, 1990), p. 81

In the two weeks between their return from Miami and Cathy's belated call to the NAACP, Frank has been a very busy man indeed, albeit off camera. He arrives home early, just in time to interrupt her call to the NAACP (Frank is always either early or late, largely for Haynes's own dramatic reasons, and even Cathy jestingly observes early on in the film, 'Big-time executive and he still can't remember a single social obligation!'). As Cathy and the children settle various domestic disagreements (whenever Cathy and the children are on screen together, she is usually scolding them), Frank sits down and disappears into the dark periwinkle blue surrounding the sofa.
It soon becomes apparent that he is crying, and as he breaks down sobbing, Janice bursts into tears, while David is terrified by the sight of his father going to pieces. Cathy sends the children to their rooms. When they are alone, Frank delivers his 'I've fallen in love ... with someone who wants to be with me' speech, adding, between sobs, 'I just – I never knew ... what it was like ... I know how cruel that sounds ...', to which Cathy responds with her strangely decisive 'I assume then ... you'll be wanting a divorce?'

We may share Cathy's shock at this announcement, for she has been quite unambiguously 'implicated', in Eve Kosofsky Sedgwick's phrase, in Frank's astonishing confession. But we are still unaware of

In the crepuscular gloom of the Whitaker sofa, Frank outs himself to Cathy

the extraordinary route Frank must have taken to arrive at this moment, and the complicated footwork it would have involved. It seems unlikely that anything could have happened in the Miami hotel room, although Frank and Blond Boy will probably at least have kissed, either before or after ascertaining each other's names. They will have agreed to remain in contact, and surely must have spoken in the two weeks since. For Frank to make such an impassioned declaration of romantic intent, they must have had a whirlwind romance during that fortnight. Moreover, unless Blond Boy also lives in Hartford or nearby, this would surely have involved further assignations, during which they must have also discussed in detail how Blond Boy – still seemingly a part of the family we saw in the Miami scenes – and Frank the Family Man can extricate themselves from their families to be together. This all, of course, takes place off screen to the sequence of events in Haynes's highly selective narrative, but its discussion here is not entirely extraneous: if we are to suspend disbelief, we must have a plausible explanation of why Frank makes his announcement at that moment.

Far From Heaven appears to be actor Nicholas 'Blond Boy' Joy's first and so far only film role. He is frequently confused with the late actor Nicholas Joy (1884–1964, seen in Jules Dassin's The

Naked City, among others) on many internet film databases. But *Far From Heaven*'s Nicholas Joy appears young enough to be his new lover's son (born in 1954, Dennis Quaid was forty-seven when filming *Far From Heaven*), which will only complicate their relationship's public face still further. Unless they choose to pass as father and son, and successfully carry out this deceit, their very decision to check into that hotel and be seen together in public could see both up on a morals charge. This, again, refers to events off screen, and invites us (or this viewer at least) to consider their fate beyond the end credits, as Haynes has confessed he intended us to, but it remains a narrative anomaly when he has publicly stated that suspension of disbelief is crucial to the success of the film.

Even though the cinema viewer is often unaware of the passage of time in a movie, all of this happens within the space of a fortnight in Haynes's narrative, and without Cathy suspecting a thing. Elision and the telescoping of timeframes are common in any narrative work, although the novel is at least expected to explain its cute narrative twists and turns. Here, Haynes moves a whole chunk of his story off screen and off limits, unbeknown even to the viewer, who has previously enjoyed a privileged knowledge of events in *Far From Heaven*. The curiosity here is not so much the lengthy elision, as the fact that Haynes then dumps the problem onto the crepuscular blue gloom of the Whitaker sofa, giving Cathy her cue to make an offer of divorce. Is Cathy stunned, relieved or perhaps, again in a convention of the genre, merely displaying the stoic martyrdom of the sort exhibited by Bette Davis's Charlotte Vale in *Now, Voyager* (1942)?

Even more curious still is the fact that a mere fortnight earlier, Cathy and Frank had in essence renewed their marriage vows over champagne at the stroke of midnight on New Year's Eve in Miami. Now, their marriage is on the rocks, steered there solely by Frank's impressive behind-the-scenes machinations. In Sirk's era, of course, such an admission would have been impossible, the ramifications vast and only hinted at here in *Far From Heaven*, and perhaps Cathy's oddly cool reaction is an example of Marcia Landy's idea of the film being 'cast in the historical context of the 1950s but contaminated by the present'. In Sirk's day, such a transgression would have to have been coded as a descent into madness, alcoholism, murder or worse, while the reactions of those around would have been equally melodramatic. Here, in the arboreal half-light of the Whitaker lounge, Cathy responds with a shocking matter-of-factness that goes straight to the point and even offers a solution: divorce, then.

As Eve Kosofsky Sedgwick suggests, the most common reaction when a husband comes out to his wife as 'gay', apart from anger or disbelief, is for the wife to feel somehow implicated in the husband's actions, often 'blaming' herself for driving him into someone else's arms. Homosexuality has already been broached early on in *Far From Heaven*, when Eleanor announces the visit of the toad-like art dealer Farnsworth, who is, as she puts it in the code of the times, 'light on his feet' (i.e. queer). Eleanor declares, 'Call me old-fashioned, but I like the men I'm around to be all men.' When she presses Cathy on her interest in the topic, Cathy lies again, saying 'I read an article recently. In a magazine.' And when Eleanor actually names the love that dare not speak its name, Cathy shudders at '*That* word.' Clearly, even though she – like us – has been excluded from Frank's 'therapy' sessions with Dr Bowman, it is a word that has been playing on her mind. And now here it is, in person, sitting on her sofa, sobbing, telling her that her life with her husband is over. Certainly, it's no way to treat a lady, although the history of cinema shows that film is no respecter of a lady's feelings.

Perhaps ultimately, *Far From Heaven* will not withstand close textual analysis, or, perhaps more accurately, Haynes has constructed the film in a way that it resists such examination. It invites us to read the narrative as conventional melodrama, while subverting any such satisfactory reading with the devices we have seen Haynes borrowing from other genres, media and theories of narrativity. Famously, or at least according to Tom Dardis in his book on writers in Hollywood, *Some Time in the Sun*, Howard Hawks told William Faulkner and his co-writers on *The Big Sleep* that as long as they kept the story moving at a clip, audiences wouldn't notice that none of it made any sense.[27] If we can allow Hawks to throw away the rule book on classical narrativity, then perhaps we can also allow Todd Haynes to ditch a few of its chapters as well.

Eleven

'I've learned my lesson about mixing with other worlds. And I've seen the sparks fly ...'

Raymond

As if Haynes's almost Hitchcockian mistreatment of his leading lady wasn't bad enough, there is yet more bad news awaiting Cathy Whitaker. When Sybil finally plucks up the courage to tell her that 'the little coloured girl that got hit' was Raymond's daughter, Cathy is distraught: 'Oh, that dear, sweet little girl. How in God's name, Sybil, could you not have told me this?'

This disclosure leads Cathy to make only her third volitional journey out of the house in the entire film, driving to Raymond's house, into a dark night to see how Sarah is, an errand that Sybil clearly believes either improper or even dangerous ('You're going there *now*?'), quoting her namesake in *The Reckless Moment*: 'Do you want me to go with you?' Raymond, of course, lives on the wrong side of the tracks, although for Cathy as much as him, there is no *right* side of the tracks in Hartford. Scorned by white society, regarded as at best trouble and at worst white trash in black society, Cathy has become a modern-day equivalent of Hawthorne's Hester Prynne in *The Scarlet Letter*, although here the scarlet letter is N, in its various uncapitalised meanings.

When she arrives at Raymond's house, the camera her attending angel at the end of its crane, the windows are boarded up against more attacks by his neighbours and Raymond asks her to meet him

around the side, where they will not be observed. It is clear from both his tone and his demeanour that Raymond is going away: 'Seems to be the one place where whites and coloureds are in full harmony. Anyway, we'll be out of here soon enough, once and for all.' After the attack on Sarah and the sudden, if unexplained, collapse of his business ('The business is through. No one's gonna hire me'), he is selling up and moving to Baltimore. As Cathy asks, 'You're moving?', Haynes has a solitary train horn hoot forlornly in the distance.

In an echo of *her* historic model, Jane Wyman's conciliatory Cary Scott in the final reels of *All That Heaven Allows*, Cathy tentatively suggests, 'Perhaps I could come for a visit … it looks as if I'm going to be single again.' Daringly, almost imploringly, she adds, 'No one would know us there.' Raymond lets her down as gently as he can: 'I'm just not sure it would be a wise idea, after everything that's— ' and he tails off. As they make their polite goodbyes, Raymond says, 'Have a proud life. A splendid life. Will you do that? Goodbye, Cathy.' For the first and only time in the film, he kisses her, gently, and on the hand.

This is in fact only the second of the two real kisses in the entire film, beyond the pecks-on-cheeks and air-kisses with which the ladies of white Hartford negotiate their social lives. The other, equally

Raymond asks Cathy to meet him by the side of the house, where rock-throwing neighbours won't see them

tellingly, is the passionate kiss between Frank and his anonymous pick-up when Cathy discovers them in Frank's office. With that chaste kiss on Cathy's hand, Raymond is no longer the Lancelot to her Guinevere, but a medieval troubadour poet bidding adieu to the object of his courtly love. Raymond may have indeed seen the sparks fly, both literal and metaphorical, in the attacks on his daughter and his house, and in the two almost rhyming 'Boy!' sequences. In the first of these, an African-American friend at Eagan's chastises him for

Raymond is leaving on a southbound train, and Haynes is about to sound the hooter; that chaste kiss, only the second of just two in the entire film

fooling around with a white woman and calls him 'boy' in the
process. In the second, a passing white businessman sees Raymond
touch Cathy's arm during their conversation outside the Ritz cinema
and yells: 'Hey! Boy! Hands off!'

At this juncture, it is worth considering just how far Cathy and
indeed Todd Haynes have come from the original thesis of *Far From
Heaven*. If the narrative is meant to be read literally and not as a
kabuki play of filmic gestures, it would seem that Cathy, her world in

'Boy' sequence, take one: a friend remonstrates with Raymond at Eagan's; 'Boy'
sequence, take two: an upstanding citizen puts Raymond in his place

tatters, is prepared to propose that she and Raymond (and Sarah) flee Hartford to live as a (presumably unmarried) mixed-race couple and family in a large anonymous city where 'no one would know us'.

By this time, Haynes has strayed so far from the partial borrowings from *All That Heaven Allows* that he allows Cathy to be betrayed or abandoned not just once but twice. After that sort of treatment, a sensible girl would consider entering a nunnery. For all the trials and tribulations that Cary and Ron are put through in Sirk's original, Sirk actually ditches the idea of the trick 'impossible' happy ending and hands the couple exactly that. With Ron recuperating on the sofa after his fall, Cary rushes to be by his side. Stirring from his concussion, Ron asks, 'You've come home?' and Cary's last words in the film are, 'Yes, darling, I've come home.' As if the point needs elaborating, Sirk summons a woodland sprite in the form of a young buck deer peering in from the snowy scene outside almost as though blessing their reunion. Corny as Kansas in August, yes, but beautiful.

Cathy, by the starkest contrast imaginable, is now facing an uncertain future as an unemployed single parent about to be divorced from a husband whose career prospects may well preclude the possibility of alimony.

Lit like a hallucination, Cathy says goodbye

There is an intriguing alternative ending to *Far From Heaven*, beyond the dialogue-free farewell scene at the railway station, but one that will never be seen by any audience. At some point in working on the script, Haynes envisioned the film ending with a voiceover from Cathy, but for reasons unknown, this also failed to make it into the final cut. Perhaps it was too pat, or obvious, too melodramatic; or maybe it was because for the first time, it gave a voice to Cathy's interior feelings that Haynes, preferring ambiguity to closure, has withheld during the film, preferring to leave the audience to guess her emotions from the cryptic glances and silent pauses of Julianne Moore's performance. (In fact, in the Q&A short that accompanies the DVD release of *Far From Heaven*, Haynes says the film is, as it were, open-plan, and one that invites the audience to project their analyses onto the characters.)

The now-abandoned voiceover begins as Cathy turns away from the sight of Raymond's disembodied hand protruding from the carriage door in a spooky farewell as the train leaves the station:

'That was the day I stopped believing in the wild ardour of things. Perhaps in love, as well. That kind of love.'

Read his lips: so does Raymond

Semaphore for what might have been; hands retracted, resignation descends; Cathy turns and walks back towards her future

The voiceover follows Cathy out of the station and towards her baby-blue-and-white 1956 Chevrolet:

'The love in books and films. The love that tells us to abandon our lives and plans, all for one brief touch of Venus.'

Cathy climbs into her car and prepares to drive away under those suspicious white blossoms:

'So often we fail in that kind of love. The world just seems too fragile a place for it. Or perhaps it's only we who are too fragile.'

Haynes's alternative ending closes with the script note that 'Spring has arrived.' Despite the meteorological incongruities in *Far From Heaven*, that early spring has arrived too late for Cathy. As the end credits roll, she is driving back to her dream home, alone, where she will willingly lock herself in again, and the weather forecast looks bleak. She has, as Haynes has said elsewhere, speaking of the characters of Fassbinder but, by extension, his own and those of Sirk, 'buckled under the pressures of society'.[28]

The crane camera has already got her as she leaves the station. Cue booby-trapped white blossoms ...

Twelve

'Sirk has made the tenderest films I know. They are the films of someone who loves people and doesn't despise them as we do.'

Rainer Werner Fassbinder, 'Fassbinder on Sirk', *Film Comment*, no. 6 (November–December 1975), p. 22

While most people might want to disassociate themselves from the wilful projection at the end of Fassbinder's second sentence there, in an interview with *Film Comment* magazine, it is a remarkable lowering of the defences by a man widely regarded as one of the most thoroughgoing misanthropes in the history of cinema.

Sirk, Fassbinder and Haynes might seem an unusual *ménage à trois*, but the connections are there. Fassbinder also used *All That Heaven Allows* as the springboard for his 1974 film *Angst essen Seele auf* (*Ali: Fear Eats the Soul*). While Haynes only began his 'official' film career in 1987, the year that Sirk died in self-imposed exile in Switzerland, Fassbinder's life overlapped with that of Sirk to the extent that during the latter's exile from a Hollywood he loathed, the two men became good friends. At one point, Fassbinder even persuaded Sirk to teach film in Hamburg.

Haynes stumbled on the work of both directors when studying film at Brown University, prior to switching courses to major in arts and semiotics. He has spoken at length of his admiration for Fassbinder, not least in Robert Fischer's short documentary, *A Powerful Political Potential: Todd Haynes on Fassbinder and Melodrama* (2006). In it, he comments on Sirk's 'Brechtian curiosity about how to critique American culture', and how Sirk's films themselves 'self-critique American society'. (Haynes cites Brecht twice in the short interview, suggesting that we may be on the right track here.) The title of Fischer's documentary comes from a comment Haynes makes about Fassbinder's identification of 'a powerful political potential in melodrama', a potential more compelling than the explicitly political films that Fassbinder's contemporaries were making in the 1970s.

Haynes told *Independent Film Quarterly*:

I was first exposed to Fassbinder's films in college and they've remained really central to my life and my inspiration. I just think he is a remarkable figure in post-war cinema and obviously, particularly, post-war German film and the New German Cinema. But he is this rare entity and seemingly becomes more so as every year passes as he belongs to a tradition of politics and social criticism in film-making, having a strong point of view that challenges the status quo, which has faded somewhat from mainstream films. He was definitely formed by '68, Europe, and a certain intellectual, progressive and political sensibility.[29]

Beyond the Oberhausen Manifesto of 1962, in which the likes of Alexander Kluge declared the death of old German cinema and the birth of the German new wave, and given the subsequent career trajectories of the likes of Herzog and Wenders, the New German Cinema movement might in retrospect be seen as a brief and illusory moment in cinema history – almost as brief and illusory as the New Queer Cinema that Haynes is credited with helping to create. But for a few years at the beginning of the 1970s, Germany was a hotbed of film-makers intent on raking over the still-glowing coals of the nation's recent past.

Chief among them was the leather-jacketed bad boy Fassbinder. In a career that often seemed fuelled by splenetic rage at the hypocrisy of postwar Germany, Fassbinder spat out some forty cinema and television films in the fifteen years of his short and incendiary career. *Fear Eats the Soul* is probably one of the most enduring of them all, and, to borrow his chosen adjectival for Sirk, the tenderest. Borrowing from both *All That Heaven Allows* and *Imitation of Life*, it pits the mismatched interracial love between an ageing cleaner and her younger Moroccan lover against both wider German society, which Fassbinder saw as irredeemably racist, and, in particular, the woman's immensely disagreeable immediate family (including Fassbinder himself as one of the sons) and neighbours. Notably, however, Fassbinder – notorious for killing off his protagonists and sending audiences home in despair – here sides with Sirk in *All That Heaven Allows*, and, despite all he puts them through, ends the film with Emmi and Ali reunited and in love. True, it's a far cry from Cary, Ron and the young buck deer, but it's also a much happier ending than anything on offer to the central trio in *Far From Heaven*.

In Robert Fischer's documentary, Haynes reveals that he admires Fassbinder because 'he opted for the popular form over the political form as a means of critique', and because he saw 'allusion, artifice and narrative as a way to get to the truth'. Although he disavows any direct influence from the director's work, Haynes says Fassbinder 'represents a general spirit that influences me'. (Interestingly, and perhaps even amusingly, Fassbinder himself, talking about Sirk to *Film Comment* magazine in 1975, declared that 'Small-town America is the last place in the world I would want to go.'[30])

It is also clear that Haynes felt that both Sirk and Fassbinder employed melodrama to present a more 'powerful' social critique than that offered by more polemical film-makers (unsurprisingly, he cites Godard as the ringleader among the latter). Yet as far as I can tell, the furthest Haynes has gone in discussing the notion of social critique in *Far From Heaven* was in a public Q&A interview when he said, 'There's *almost* no subtext [his italics]. Everything in this film is on the surface.' That 'almost', at least, gives us some room for manoeuvre. And his insistence that in the film, 'what you see is what you get' might actually be his way of saying that the surface itself is critique enough.

Fassbinder and Sirk would be just two of the influences that Haynes brought to the heady stew that became known as the 'New Queer Cinema', the movement identified and christened by critic and cultural theorist B. Ruby Rich in her 1992 *Sight & Sound* article, 'Homo Pomo: The New Queer Cinema'.[31] While others such as Gus van Sant and Gregg Araki would introduce queer readings of the road movie, the buddy movie and other forms, Haynes was by far the most movie-literate of his queer contemporaries. Like the unashamedly low-budget and low-rent Bruce LaBruce, who began his career as editor of the queer punk fanzine *J.D.s*, Haynes was a child of the post-punk era, but one versed in the work of Kenneth Anger, Jack Smith, Curt McDowell, Rosa von Praunheim and Frank Ripploh. He had a taste for trashy television, from *I Love Lucy* to *The Twilight Zone*, but also, as that early student film on Rimbaud suggested, a highly developed sense of queer aesthetics, from Jean Genet's writings and his only film, *Un Chant d'amour* (1950), which inspired the 'Homo' section of *Poison*, to the Super-8 queer poetics of Derek Jarman, not least in *Jubilee* (1978), *The Angelic Conversation* (1985), *The Last of England* (1988), *The Garden* (1990) and others. All these would collide in what B. Ruby Rich saw as one of the defining moments of New Queer Cinema, Haynes's pyrotechnic first feature, *Poison*, although just eight years later, Rich would declare New Queer Cinema to be 'over'.[32] Where – or indeed whether – *Far From Heaven* sits in the spectrum of New Queer Cinema is a topic that is still being debated, some time, even, after the hubbub around his subsequent film, *I'm Not There*, died down.

Thirteen

Tragedy seems paradoxically to have been the favoured tone of much of the New Queer Cinema.

B. Ruby Rich, 'Queer and Present Danger', *Sight & Sound*,
vol. 10 no. 3 (March 2000), p. 22

By that definition alone, *Far From Heaven* ought to walk off with the Lifetime Achievement award at the Queer Oscars, although B. Ruby

Rich has problematised its nomination. In passing, she also points up the enduring power of tragedy, and its appeal to a cinematic movement that wanted to take its audience by the lapels and give them a good shaking. When she returned to her theme, in 2000, Rich wrote that

from the beginning the New Queer Cinema was a more successful term for a moment than a movement. It was meant to catch the beat of a new kind of film- and video-making that was fresh, edgy, low-budget, inventive, unapologetic, sexy and stylistically daring.[33]

Perhaps taking van Sant's *My Own Private Idaho* (1991), Araki's *The Living End* (1992) and Kalin's *Swoon* (1992) as givens, Rich identified only a handful of other films with that initial 'moment' of New Queer Cinema, among them Isaac Julien's *Young Soul Rebels* (1991), Hettie McDonald's *Beautiful Thing* (1996) and Rose Troche's *Go Fish* (1994). Rich wrote:

The work spawned a whole sector of queer filmdom, not just genres but viewers and distributors and venues. By the late 90s there were well over 100 film festivals billed as queer; according to one survey, a full 80 per cent of the work shown there was never seen outside the queer circuit.[34]

New Queer Cinema, Rich suggested, was a victim of its own success, unleashing a flood of lesser material to a dwindling and jaded audience. Briefly, New Queer Cinema was, if not quite hot box office, then definitely very warm box office. Some directors, such as van Sant with *Even Cowgirls Get the Blues* (1993), *Good Will Hunting* (1997) and, most recently, *Milk* (2008), found mainstream success, as did *Gods and Monsters* (1998) director-writer Bill Condon with his stage-to-screen adaptations of *Chicago* (2002) and *Dreamgirls* (2006). Others such as LaBruce (most recently with *Otto: Or, Up with Dead People* [2008]) and Araki (with his 'Teenage Apocalypse' trilogy [1993–7] and the later *Mysterious Skin* [2004]) stuck to their indie guns. Some, such as Troche, Kalin and Jenny Livingston (*Paris Is Burning* [1990]), seemed to all but disappear – although both Kalin (with *Savage Grace* [2007]) and Troche (*The Safety of Objects* [2001]) have made more conventional films since – or realign their talents in other directions.

As with other irruptions of 'queer' culture, such as the now-defunct Queer Nation activist group, and the musical genres of Queercore, Riot Grrrl and Homocore/cult, New Queer Cinema was the product of a particular period and, Rich believes, a particular set of tensions. Notable among these was the fact that some of these young film-makers were or had been involved in ACT UP, its creative offshoot Gran Fury, the lesbian/feminist video collective DIVA and other queer-identified groups besides. She also cites the furore on the American far right over the state funding that went into Haynes's *Poison* as a contributory factor in defining the movement in its moment.

While queer theory continues to proliferate in academia faster than the Andromeda Strain, and the word still attaches itself, with diminishing impact, to book titles, it has lost 'traction' in day-to-day use. Many homosexuals found the word 'queer' retrograde and even offensive, while others continue to use it to distance themselves from the baggage that comes with the word 'gay': white, male, middle class, and a whole host of other negative connotations besides. To many, however, 'queer' was a long-overdue return to the fighting talk of the original Gay Liberation Front, whose spirit might be found today in the guerrilla antics of San Francisco's wittily named Gay Shame street activists.

Rich saw the New Queer Cinema as fragmenting, its engines failing before it had even begun its trajectory. The queerest film she could conjure up in 2000 was the serially heterosexual Spike Jonze's *Being John Malkovich*, which might see Rich aligning herself with the Homocore/cult manifesto's tenet that you didn't have to be queer to be, well, queer. She asserted, 'Lacking the concentrated creative presence and focused community responsiveness of the past, the New Queer Cinema has become just another niche market.'[35]

Looking back at the careers of some of the key figures of that moment, it is difficult to identify a more wilful, contrarian and mischievous talent than Haynes. Even his commercial or critical failures, such as *Velvet Goldmine* – one of the few films to challenge Nicolas Roeg's *Performance* (1970) for the title of most perversely inventive pop movie ever made – are works that reward repeated viewing. And whatever the final tally on its box office, the later *I'm Not There* may well come to be regarded as a polysemous masterpiece.

None of which, however, answers an earlier question set here: Is *Far From Heaven* queer, post-queer, none of the above? Both Tom Kalin and Gregg Araki had 'done' genre before: Kalin with *Swoon*, which took the covert homosexual subtext of Hitchcock's *Rope* (1948) and made it overt; and Araki with *The Living End*, the HIV buddy/road movie that flew in the face of polite discourse on AIDS and entered the territory of *Bonnie and Clyde* (1967) and *Badlands* (1973). Nothing in either Queer Cinema or Haynes's own canon could have prepared the viewer for what he did in *Far From Heaven* (at the time of writing, we have no indication of how he is planning to approach his TV series remake of *Mildred Pierce* for HBO).

When it first became known that Haynes was planning to make a film based on the works or era of Sirk, it seemed likely that Bruce LaBruce might put a price on his head for what sounded like treason against the queer manifesto. In hindsight, however, *Far From Heaven* might in fact be the cleverest and, if we're still allowed to say it, coolest move that any of the New Queer Cinema upstarts could have made.

From a queer perspective, with *Far From Heaven* Haynes pulled off a number of political, theoretical and cinematic coups. He fashioned a simulacrum of the Sirkian melodrama that could have been read as the real thing and which, like Menard's *Quixote*, was at the same time both identical yet totally different. He concocted a 'women's film' that played all the emotional keys of that genre while simultaneously managing to upend most of its conventions. While seeming to align itself to audience expectations, it also resisted the demands that the audience usually makes of the genre, not least the 'happy' ending. It may sound somewhat flippant, but he has created what might be called a pre-feminist post-feminist film, adopting the camouflage of an earlier, pre-liberation era, entirely bypassing the 'empowering' notions of so-called 'second-wave' feminism, and arriving at a 'third-wave' feminism of the sort found in the linguistic and psychoanalytical theories of Hélène Cixous and Julia Kristeva. In more down-to-earth terms, he goes beyond even the freewheeling existentialism of *Thelma and Louise* (1991) to produce a film which, despite its director's insistence on the primacy of appearance, is deeply melancholic and, in the abjection of its leading female character, almost as cruel as Lars von Trier's *Breaking the Waves* (1996).

Similarly, and this may well seem equally arch, he has also contrived to make a pre-'gay' post-'gay' movie, using a few devices he borrowed from Fassbinder, and others besides. Here too, Haynes skips nimbly across eras and genres, from the coded homophile films of the 1950s, through the hand-wringing apologias of the 60s, bypassing Hollywood's brief honeymoon with 'nice' homos in the 70s and 80s entirely, and reappearing in the post-gay 2000s, when he and his compatriots set about torching a few decades of gay cinema history with the bratty tactics that so thrilled B. Ruby Rich (and quite a few of the rest of us besides). New Queer Film, like queer theory in general, had no truck with Nice; as one of Queer's slogans had it, 'Just because you're gay, doesn't make it OK'. Here, in the manner of Fassbinder's controversial treatment of queers in *Fox and His Friends* (1975) and other films, Haynes presents Frank as an all-too-human figure – insecure, selfish, dishonest, cowardly, weak. Moreover, he represents Frank's manifold failings couched in a genre piece of a kind that is widely regarded as a mainstay of 'gay' culture, the 1950s weepie. This, however, is a 1950s weepie bristling with devices borrowed from half a century of European and American avant-garde film and the critical theory that supplied the commentary along the way.

The outdated notion of the Hollywood weepie as an integral part of 'gay' culture – an idea that many queers regard as just another monkey on their backs, along with light opera, pink jumpers and Judy Garland records – also leads us to the concept of 'camp' in *Far From Heaven*. After Sandy Powell's dresses and Haynes's own design for the title font, the campest thing here is probably Elmer Bernstein's score.

Despite a career spanning half a century and dotted with Oscars,[36] Bernstein never actually scored a film in Sirk's genre. He leapt at the chance to work on *Far From Heaven*, calling it his favourite project in fifteen years, 'the kind of score you don't hear any more', and his last to make it to the screen before he died in 2004. The result is a knowing, perhaps even ironic, reimagining of the weepie soundtrack, a musical form that Bernstein actually had little time for, either then or now. He outlined his own opinion of the genre quite forcefully to the *Guardian*'s Stuart Jeffries at the time of the film's release:

I was around in the 1950s and I didn't go look at these films. We called them weepies, and they weren't our kind of thing at all. We were into dark, cutting-edge movies, not pictures for women with Rock Hudson in them.[37]

This might make Bernstein an odd choice for composer on a film like *Far From Heaven*, but Haynes says that they bonded like family. Without recourse to pastiche or parody, Bernstein's *Far From Heaven* score was 'just trying to be true to the emotions in the film'.[38]

Yet, considered in the light of the definitions laid down in Sontag's defining essay 'Notes on "Camp"', *Far From Heaven* actually disqualifies itself from almost every category that she regarded as the essence of camp ('It goes without saying', wrote Sontag, in just one of her definitions, 'that the Camp sensibility is disengaged, depoliticized – or at least apolitical'[39]). In fact, everything that Haynes and his collaborators have said about the film militates against a reading of *Far From Heaven* as camp.

Perhaps we – and Haynes – have the dour influence of Fassbinder to thank for that.

The great German miserablist Fassbinder deliberately courted controversy throughout most of his career, but was just as likely to find himself under attack from the left as from the right, and often for his bleak – and utterly politically incorrect – portrayal of his characters. Frank's woebegone life in the closet (which, as Haynes's camera pointedly underlines, has taken him to the brink of alcoholism) is the stuff of 'problem' films such as *Victim* (1961), although Haynes appears to offer him a thoroughly modern, happy ending, even though the scenery may already be starting to wobble in that hotel scene. This could in fact be the one trick 'happy' ending in the film: Frank is about to embark on a terrifyingly steep learning curve when he and Blond Boy quit their hotel room, and it is hard to imagine how they might survive, either as individuals or a 'couple', after the screen goes blank. In fact, if we were to extrapolate into Frank's future, it might involve another encounter with the cops, arraignment and jail time. Whereas Cathy has offered to volunteer for the NAACP, you get the sense that Frank isn't going to be making a similar offer to the Mattachine Society any time soon. The fate that Haynes seems to imply could be lying in wait for Frank beyond the end credits is likely to be as bleak as the one Fassbinder showed us on screen in *Fox and His Friends*, with the queer Everyman Franz Biberkopf betrayed, abandoned and dead.

While the queer narrative is left hanging in mid-air in that hotel room, the issue of race departs on a southbound train for New York and Washington, with Raymond and Sarah heading for Baltimore and an uncertain future (a decade later, it will experience ten days of uncontainable race riots in the wake of the assassination of Martin Luther King). However far the ripples from the attack on Sarah and the thwarted friendship between Cathy and Raymond might spread, Hartford will probably go back to sleep, its prejudices not only intact but reaffirmed by recent events. But, then, the last thing Haynes wants to offer here is film as moral exemplar. And yet ...

Fourteen

'The big, dominant, grand crises of American culture, which I don't think
have gone away, are the predominant themes of this movie.'

Todd Haynes, *The Making of 'Far From Heaven'*, TV documentary,
Andrew Bernard/Danny Miller (KG Productions, 2002)

... perhaps he does.

If the 'big, dominant, grand crises of American culture' that
Haynes speaks of are race and sexuality, then we have to admit that
Hollywood has been here before, although with very mixed results.
It can at least be said to have acquitted itself on the issue of racism on
many occasions, in films ranging from *In the Heat of the Night*
(1967) to *Mississippi Burning* (1988), even though it cannot be said
to have in any way adequately addressed the subjects of
homosexuality or homophobia.

In the twenty-first century, with the murders in 1998 of James
Byrd Jr and Matthew Shepard still fresh in the memory, it would be a
bald truism to say that racism and homophobia still persist in the
United States (Byrd was chained by his feet to the back of a truck by
racists and dragged along Texas back roads until his head and an arm
were severed; Shepard was pistol-whipped unconscious by
queerbashers, crucified on a fence in the wilds of Wyoming and left
there to die). But perhaps these aren't the 'grand crises' that Haynes is
referring to. Certainly, he has avoided directly addressing any Big
Politics in his films to date. As he has said of his heroes Sirk and
Fassbinder, they succeeded by using 'allusion, artifice and narrative as
a way to get to the truth'.[40] Moreover, his readings of Baudrillard and
Lyotard *et al.* must surely have led him to a more complex and subtle
understanding of the forces at work on what he has called 'people
trapped in houses and a corrupt society'.[41] Could it be, then, that
Todd Haynes has even bigger fish to fry? Is *Far From Heaven* a
philosophical treatise on spiritual anomie camouflaged as a Sunday-
afternoon-on-the-sofa two-hankie weepie?

From *Superstar* to *I'm Not There*, Haynes has always taken a tangential, elliptical approach to the subject matter seemingly at hand, focusing in on a small detail or event from an unusual angle, a tactic that might in fact allow him to smuggle an even larger elephant into the room while no one is looking. Both *Superstar* and *[safe]* can be read as critiques of a wide-ranging and pervasive malaise at the heart of North American culture; and beyond and below the surface binarisms of black/white, straight/queer, rich/poor in *Far From Heaven*, there is a distinct suggestion that everyone, even Mona Lauder and the reprehensible Farnsworth, is, in Haynes's choice of word, a 'victim' of a similar malaise. Which is why I find myself returning to the notion of 'paralysis' in Joyce's 'The Dead' when casting around for a work of art that evokes a similar philosophy.

It may seem extreme to interrogate *Far From Heaven* through the lens of postmodernism, but it seems almost impossible to imagine that Haynes came to the project without the baggage assembled during his education. A former fellow student at Brown University, Karin Brad, now a film academic in France, even published a brief memoir of their student days in an unapologetically negative review of *I'm Not There* for the *Huffington Post*. Brad described Haynes as 'the most memorable person in the class', as they chewed over Baudrillard and Lyotard while he was still working on *Superstar*: 'How inspiring this class must have been, I thought, to see its precepts executed so exactly in a two-hour plus film, 20 years later,' Brad wrote, before going on to criticise Haynes for losing sight of his student influences in *I'm Not There*:

Yet while the theorists who so influenced Haynes – Baudrillard and Lyotard – connected their analysis of the commercial proliferation of images to a critique of capitalism and use value, Haynes connects his playful deconstruction of Dylan to nothing, absolutely nothing.[42]

Whether or not you agree with Brad's opinion of *I'm Not There* isn't really the issue here, but her testimony would appear to be supporting evidence for those of us who suspect that, along with his colour swatches, Haynes was also packing *Simulacra and Simulation* and *The Postmodern Condition* in his workbag while working on this and perhaps virtually all of his other films besides. *Far From Heaven* has already inspired a small cottage industry of academic critical theory devoted to its exegesis, and this book can only skim the surface of the recondite debates over allegory, allusion, surface and interior, postmodern gameplay and intertextual ping-pong matches that continue over *Far From Heaven* and his other works.

It is also quite clear that Haynes *intended* his film to inspire speculation and debate among viewers, particularly about off-screen events and what happens after the final credits, which may go some of the way to explaining his decision to send Frank on that trip into a parallel universe for his whirlwind romance with Blond Boy. Haynes admits he was delighted when an otherwise level-headed friend confessed that she hoped, maybe even prayed, that Cathy and Raymond would at least write to each other afterwards; proof, there, that his engine for generating audience anxiety worked. We are left only with Haynes's confession, repeated on many occasions, that 'at the most basic level I wanted to make a movie that made people cry'.

The 'problem' with an open-ended film like *Far From Heaven* is that the director-writer asks each viewer to complete the film themselves. This again is nothing particularly new in the history of film. *The Big Sleep* is by no means the only film to have left viewers baffled, although there the fault in the narrative in fact lies with the original Raymond Chandler novel, which killed off Sean Regan a month before the story starts, but leaves his disappearance centre-stage (Chandler admitted that he didn't know who killed Regan, either). It also happened in *The Maltese Falcon* (1941), where the killer is identified only by a brief smile spotted in a crowd at the very beginning of the film. In a later, notorious, example of narrative wilfulness, Peter Greenaway's *The Draughtsman's Contract* (1982), 'nobody' commits the murder at the centre of the film, largely because identifying the killer wasn't the point of the film.

More recently, both Michael Haneke and Abbas Kiarostami have spoken at length about the use of elision in their work, the latter going so far as to say, 'Unfinished cinema leaves room for the audience to take part in the creative process. It allows everyone to see their own film.'[43]

This is not to compare *Far From Heaven* to any of these films or film-makers, merely to note a similarity in approach to narrative and the treatment of a chosen theme. In fashioning his ambiguous, deceptive, pre-/post-feminist/'gay' conceit on the Sirkian melodrama, and deliberately leaving the fates of the three lead characters hanging in the balance as the end credits roll, in a film that finally proves itself to be anything but an empty sign, Haynes leaves the viewer to pick up the pen of Barthes's dead Author and write the ending themselves.

Notes

1 Peter Bradshaw, 'I Came to Mock and Stayed to Pray', *Guardian*, 7 March 2003.

2 Robert Sullivan, 'This Is Not a Bob Dylan Movie', *The New York Times*, 7 October 2007.

3 Ella Taylor, 'Get Out Your Handkerchiefs', *LA Weekly*, 14 November 2002.

4 Christine Vachon, *A Killer Life* (New York: Limelight Editions, 2007), p. 1.

5 In 2007, auditors PriceWaterhouseCoopers estimated that of all US cinemagoers, Hispanics outstripped Caucasians by 20 per cent.

6 Mary Ann Doane, 'Pathos and Pathology: The Cinema of Todd Haynes', in Amelie Hastie *et al.* (eds), *Todd Haynes: A Magnificent Obsession*, special issue of *Camera Obscura* 57 (Durham, NC: Duke University Press, 2004), p. 12.

7 Lee Siegel, 'Why Does Hollywood Hate the Suburbs?', *Wall Street Journal*, 27 December 2008.

8 Marcia Landy, 'Storytelling and Information in Todd Haynes' Films', in James Morrison (ed.), *The Cinema of Todd Haynes: All That Heaven Allows* (London: Wallflower Press, 2007), p. 23.

9 Andrew Sarris, *The American Cinema* (New York: Da Capo Books, 1996), p. 109.

10 'Sirk Issue', *Screen*, Summer 1971.

11 Sarris, *American Cinema*, p. 109.

12 Todd McGowan, 'Relocating Our Enjoyment of the 1950s: The Politics of Fantasy in *Far From Heaven*', in Morrison (ed.), *Cinema of Todd Haynes*, p. 114.

13 Amy Kroin, '"Movies are nothing until we bring emotional life to them"', *Salon*, 11 November 2002. Available online at: <http://www.salon. com/entertainment/movies/int/2002/ 11/11/haynes>.

14 Todd Haynes, interview with Geoffrey O'Brien, *ArtForum*, November 2002. Available online at: <http:// artforum.com/new.php?pn=inprint& id=3653>.

15 'Harvard Professor Jailed', *The New York Times*, 20 July 2009.

16 Todd Haynes, interview with Dennis Lim, 'Heaven Sent', *Village Voice*, 29 October 2002.

17 This also involves more fancy footwork by Haynes: how does avant-garde art in a gallery become a decorative reproduction on an office wall on the other side of town?

18 Thomas Elsaesser, 'Tales of Sound and Fury: Observations on the Family Melodrama' (1972), in Barry Keith Grant (ed.), *Film Genre Reader III* (Austin: University of Texas Press, 2003), p. 366.

19 Ibid.

20 Sigmund Freud, *A Child Is Being Beaten* (London: Hogarth Press, 1955).

21 Taylor, 'Get Out Your Handkerchiefs'.

22 Scott Higgins, 'Orange and Blue, Desire and Loss: The Colour Score in *Far From Heaven*', in Morrison (ed.), *Cinema of Todd Haynes*, p. 101.

23 Ibid., p. 111.

24 Andrew O'Hehir, 'Far from Heaven', *Salon*, 8 November 2002. Available online at: <http://www.salon. com/entertainment/movies/int/2002/ 11/11/haynes>.

25 Lynne Joyrich, 'Written on the Screen: Mediation and Immersion in *Far From Heaven*', in Hastie *et al.* (eds), *Magnificent Obsession*, p. 197.

26 Ibid.

27 Tom Dardis, *Some Time in the Sun* (New York: Charles Scribner's Sons, 1976), p. 76.

28 *The Making of 'Far From Heaven'*, TV documentary, Andrew Bernard/Danny Miller (KG Productions, 2002).

29 Todd Haynes, interview with Todd Konrad, 'Considering Fassbinder', *Independent Film Quarterly*, nd. Available online at: <http://independentfilmquarterly.net/film-articles/considering-fassbinder-reflections-from-todd-h.html>.

30 Rainer Werner Fassbinder, 'Fassbinder on Sirk', *Film Comment*, no. 6 (November–December 1975), p. 22.

31 B. Ruby Rich, 'Homo Pomo: The New Queer Cinema', *Sight & Sound*, vol. 2 no. 5 (September 1992), p. 30.

32 B. Ruby Rich, 'Queer and Present Danger', *Sight & Sound*, vol. 10 no. 3 (March 2000), p. 22.

33 Ibid.

34 Ibid.

35 Ibid.

36 Think: *Man with the Golden Arm* (1955), *The Sweet Smell of Success* (1957), *Some Came Running* (1958), *The Magnificent Seven* (1960), *To Kill a Mockingbird* (1962), *Hud* (1963), and later soundtracks for *Trading Places* (1983), *Ghostbusters* (1984), *My Left Foot* (1989) and *The Grifters* (1990), although not all were Oscar winners.

37 Stuart Jeffries, 'Some You Win', *Guardian*, 6 January 2003.

38 Ibid.

39 Susan Sontag, 'Notes on "Camp"', in *Against Interpretation and Other Essays* (New York: Farrar, Straus and Giroux, 1961), p. 275.

40 *Making of 'Far From Heaven'*.

41 Ibid.

42 Karin Brad, 'I'm Not There', *Huffington Post*, 20 December 2007. Available online at: <http://www.huffingtonpost.com/karin-badt/im-not-there_b_77724.html>.

43 Abbas Kiarostami, interview with Maya Jaggi, *Guardian*, 13 June 2009.

Credits

Far From Heaven
US/2002

Directed by
Todd Haynes
Written by
Todd Haynes
Casting
Laura Rosenthal
Music
Elmer Bernstein
Costume Designer
Sandy Powell
Editor
James Lyons
Production Designer
Mark Friedberger
Director of Photography
Edward Lachman A.S.C.
Co-producers
Bradford Simpson
Declan Baldwin
Executive Producers
John Wells
Eric Robison
John Sloss
Steven Soderbergh
George Clooney
Produced by
Jody Patton
Christine Vachon

© Focus Features
© Vulcan Productions
A Killer Films – John
Wells – Section Eight
Production
A Film by Todd Haynes

Associate Editor
Shelly Westerman

Re-recording Mixers
Leslie Shatz
Marshall Garlington
**Post-production
Supervisor**
Bradley M. Goodman
**Supervising Sound
Editor**
Kelley Baker
Key Hairstylist
Alan D'Angerio
Hair Stylist
Michael Kriston
Make-up Supervisor
Elaine Offers
Make-up Artist
Hildie Ginsberg
Art Director
Peter Rogness
Assistant Art Directors
Jeff McDonald
Miguel Lopez-Castillo
Product Placement
Annie Young
Researcher
Sheri Von Seeberg
Graphics
Holly Watson
Set Decorator
Ellen Christiansen
Leadman
Tim Metzger
Set Dresser Foreman
Harvey Goldberg
On-set Dresser
JoAnn Atwood
Assistant Set Decorator
Rena DeAngelo
**Art Department
Coordinator**
Claire Kirk

**Art Department
Production Assistant**
Alex DiGerlando
Set Dressers
Henry Kaplan
Janine Pesce
Joanna Hartell
Roman Greller
**Assistant Costume
Designer**
Lisa Padovani
Wardrobe Supervisors
Susan J. Wright
David Davenport
Costume Coordinator
M. J. McGrath
Costume Assistant
Jessica Jahn
Costumers
Patricia Eiben
Tom Stokes
Barbara Presar
Set Costumers
Tom Soluri
Cheryl Kilbourne-
Kimpton
Jill E. Anderson
Tailors
Joni M. Huth
Dain I. Kalas
Production Coordinator
Koula Sossiadis
**Assistant Production
Coordinator**
Rhonda George
**Second Second
Assistant Director**
Kristal D. Moseley
**Key Production
Assistant**
Dave Glew

Production Secretary
Katina Sossiadis
Office Production
Assistant
J. Eric Fisher
Ryan Lakenan
Production Office
Interns
Cheyanne M. Casey
Conrad L. Tamayo
Kenda Greenwood
Rich Cairns
Brett Spiegel
Assistant to Mr Haynes
Slats Grobnik
Checkers Smith
Assistant to Ms
Vachon
Daniel Wagner
Assistant to Ms Moore
Reshma Gopaldas
Assistant to Mr Quaid
Beau Holden
Set Production
Assistants
Debbie Stampfle
Mike Currie
Erica Levy
Derek Wimble
Set Interns
Daniel Garrison
Zerlina Oppenheim
Ray Negron
Lindsay Feldman
Katie Feola
Sebastian Ischer
Film Runners
Daniel Winchester
Raynelle Mensah
Camera Operator
Craig Haagensen

First Assistant Camera
Richard Gioia
Second Assistant
Camera
Jay Feather
Loader
Anthony Hechanova
Script Supervisor
Thomas Johnston
Production Sound Mixer
Drew Kunin
Boom Operators
Joseph White, Jr
Jeanne L. Gilliland
Still Photographers
David Lee
Abbott Genzer
Location Manager
Mike S. Ryan
Assistant Location
Manager
Kellie Morrison
Location Production
Assistants
Jesse Hove
David Chambers
Location Coordinator
Ana Lombardo
Location Assistants
Kip Myers
Christine Leaman
April Taylor
Joaquin Diego Prange
Location Scout
Kieran Shea
Location Intern
Anabel Manchester
Parking Coordinator
Edward Tejada
Gaffer
John W. Deblau

Best Boy Electric
David Franzoni
3rd Electric
Mark Schwentner
Rigging Best Boy
Richard Ford
Generator Operator
Charles Meere III
Rigging Gaffer
Thomas Percarpio
Shop Electric
Paul Kinghan
Key Grip
James C. McMillan III
Best Boy Grip
David F. Lowry, Jr
Grips
James C. McMillan, Jr
Chris Vaccaro
Divine T. Cox
Dolly Grip
Rick Marroquin
Key Rigging Grip
Craig Vaccaro
Rigging Grip
Nick Vaccaro
Property Master
Sandy Hamilton
Assistant Property
Master
Kris Moran
Picture Vehicle
Coordinator
Thomas C. Allen
Special Effects
Coordinator
Steve Kirshoff
Special Effects
Assistants
Thomas L. Viviano
Michael Bird

**Process and Rear
Screen Projection**
William G. Hansard
Don Hansard, Jr
**Construction
Coordinator**
Nick Miller
Key Shop Craft
Gordon Krause
Shop Craft
Douglas M. Bowen
Paul Divone
Roger Lang
Jeff Lomaglio
Tim Main
Malcolm Reid
Richard A. Sirico
Thomas White
Derrick Alford
Marcial Garlitos
Steven A. Lawler
Ronald Miller
James Maiello
James Sadek
Robert A. Vaccariello
1st Greensperson
Will Scheck
2nd Greensperson
Mark Selemon
Greenspersons
Romano Pugliese
Jonathan Swain
Orchestration
Emilie A. Bernstein
Assistant Orchestration
Patrick Russ
Piano Solos
Cynthia Millar
Music Editors
Joe Lisanti
Joanie Diener M.P.S.E.

Scoring Engineer
Dan Wallin

Score recorded at
Warner Bros. scoring
stage
Title design Marlene
McCarty for BUREAU
Paintings Bruno Jakob
Titles and opticals
Custom Film Effects
(Mark Dornfeld, Susan
Shin George)

CAST
Julianne Moore
Cathy Whitaker
Dennis Quaid
Frank Whitaker
Dennis Haysbert
Raymond Deagan
Patricia Clarkson
Eleanor Fine
Viola Davis
Sybil
James Rebhorn
Dr Bowman
Bette Henritze
Mrs Leacock
Michael Gaston
Stan Fine
Ryan Ward
David Whitaker
Lindsay Andretta
Janice Whitaker
Jordan Puryear
Sarah Deagan
Kyle Smyth
Billy Hutchinson
Celia Weston
Mona Lauder

Barbara Garrick
Doreen
Olivia Birkelund
Nancy
Stevie Ray Dallimore
Dick Dawson
Mylika Davis
Esther
Jason Franklin
Photographer
Gregory Marlow
Reginald Carter
C. C. Loveheart
Marlene
June Squibb
Elderly woman
Laurent Giroux
Man with moustache
Alex Santoriello
Spanish bartender
Matt Malloy
Red-faced man
J. B. Adams
Maurice Farnsworth
Kevin Carrigan
Soda jerk
Chance Kelly
Tall man
Declan Baldwin
Officer No. 1
Brian Delate
Officer No. 2
Pamela Evans
Kitty
Joe Holt
Hotel waiter
Ben Moss
Billy Hutchinson's
friend
Susan Willis
Receptionist

Karl Schroeder
Conductor
Lance Olds
Bail clerk
Jonathan McClain
Staff Member No. 1
Nicholas Joy
Blond Boy
Virl Andrick
Kenny's father
Jezebel Montero
Hooker
Geraldine Bartlett
Woman at party
Ernest Rayford III
Glaring man
Duane McLaughlin
Jake
Betsy Aidem
Pool mother
**Mary Anna
Klindtworth**
Pool daughter

Ted Neustadt
Ron
Thomas Torres
Bandleader

Colour by CFI
The producers wish to
thank
New Jersey Motion
Picture and Television
Commission,
City of New York
Mayor's Office for Film,
Theater & Broadcasting,
City of Yonkers Mayor's
Office for Film,
New Jersey Cities and
Towns of Bayonne,
Elizabeth, Kearny,
Hackensack, Livingston,
HoHoKus North
Arlington, Cranford,
Patterson, Union City,

Bloomfield New Jersey
Public Library,
Morristown & Erie
Railway, New Jersey
Transit, The National
Association for the
Advancement of Colored
Peoples for the use of the
NAACP brochure, *The
Hartford Courant*,
Dan Frazier, Scott
Greenstein, Wendy
Haynes, Joan McAllister,
Phil Morrison, Noah
Reibel, Robin Rosenberg,
Michael Silverman,
Joanne Woodward
Special thanks to Craig
Gering, Steven Raphael
'For Bompi'

Focus Features LLC and
Vulcan Productions Inc.

Bibliography

Elsaesser, Thomas, 'Tales of Sound and Fury: Observations on the Family Melodrama' (1972), in Barry Keith Grant (ed.), *Film Genre Reader III* (Austin: University of Texas Press, 2003).

Hastie, Amelie, Lynn Joyrich, Constance Penley, Sasha Torres, Patricia White and Sharon Willis (eds), *Todd Haynes: A Magnificent Obsession*, special issue of *Camera Obscura* 57 (Durham, NC: Duke University Press, 2004).

Morrison, James (ed.), *The Cinema of Todd Haynes: All That Heaven Allows* (London: Wallflower Press, 2007).

Rich, B. Ruby, 'Queer and Present Danger', in Jim Hillier (ed.), *American Independent Cinema: A Sight and Sound Reader* (London: BFI, 2000).

——— 'The New Queer Cinema', in Harry M. Benshoff and Sean Griffin (eds), *Queer Cinema: The Film Reader* (New York: Routledge, 2004).

Sarris, Andrew, *The American Cinema* (New York: Da Capo Books, 1996).

Vachon, Christine, *A Killer Life* (New York: Limelight Editions, 2007).